THE
HEIDELBERG
CATECHISM
with Scripture Texts

THE HEIDELBERG CATECHISM
with Scripture Texts

Scripture references printed from the *New International Version.*

FAITH
ALIVE®
Christian Resources

Grand Rapids, Michigan

Faith Alive Chrisitian Resources published by CRC Publications.
Copyright © 1989 by CRC Publications, 2850 Kalamazoo SE, Grand Rapids,
Michigan 49560. All rights reserved. Printed in the United States of America.

Scripture taken from the HOLY BIBLE, NEW INTERNATIONAL VERSION.
Copyright © 1973, 1978, 1984, Internatoinal Bible Society. Used by permission of
Zondervan Bible Publishers.

Library of Congress Cataloging-in-Publication Data
Heidelberger Katechismus. English.
        The Heidelberg catechism with Scripture texts.
                p.   cm.
        "Scripture feference printed from the New International version."
        1. Reformed Church—Catechisms—English. 2. Christian Reformed
Church—Catechisms—English. I. Title.
BX9428.A3   1989
238'.42—dc19   89-30562
                                                            CIP

10 9 8 7 6

ISBN 0-930265-67-X

♻ Printed on recycled paper

Preface

From his castle in Heidelberg, Elector Frederick III ruled the most important German province, the Palatinate, from 1559 to 1576. In 1562 he commissioned the preparation of a new catechism for guiding ministers and teachers in instructing the people in the Christian faith. By the end of that year the new catechism was ready; it was approved by a synod in Heidelberg early in January and published in German with a preface by Frederick III, dated January 19, 1563. The Heidelberg Catechism, as it came to be known, is undoubtedly the most widely used and warmly praised catechism of the Reformation period.

An old tradition credits Zacharias Ursinus and Caspar Olevianus as the primary authors of the catechism. All we know for sure, however, is that the Heidelberg was a team project. In his preface, the Elector mentions no specific names but tells us that the theological faculty, the superintendents, and the chief officers of the Palatinate church all took part in the catechism's production. Of course, a team project usually relies heavily on one or two persons who prepare preliminary drafts. Most authorities believe Ursinus had this leading role in composing the Heidelberg Catechism, though some think it may have been Olevianus.

A second and third German edition appeared within a few months of the first. Each of these added a few lines to form what later came to be called the eightieth question. A fourth edition was basically the same as the third; it was included, between the forms for baptism and the Lord's Supper, in the new Palatinate Church Order published on November 15, 1563. This fourth edition is the "received text" (*textus receptus*), used by Christians throughout the world. An official Latin translation of the catechism was also published in Heidelberg in the early months of 1563.

At the Synod of Dort in 1618-1619, delegates from the Reformed churches of Europe gave the Heidelberg Catechism high praise for its pedagogical and doctrinal features. It soon became the most ecumenical of all the Reformed catechisms and confessions. The Heidelberg Catechism has been translated into most of the European languages and into many Asian and African languages as well.

In 1968 the Synod of the Christian Reformed Church (CRC) appointed a committee to prepare a new English translation of the Heidelberg Catechism, "a modern and accurate translation . . . which will serve as the official text of the Heidelberg Catechism and as a guide for catechism preaching." Since the biblical texts from the *Revised Standard Version* (RSV) were to be used in this new translation of the catechism, synod appointed another committee to review the biblical passages referred to in the various answers. The final text of the new English translation, with the approved biblical references, was adopted by the CRC Synod of 1975.

In 1986 the CRC synod appointed a new committee to work on changing the biblical references in the catechism to the *New International Version* (NIV)— and to recommend changes in the catechism's text made necessary by this revision. Synod also directed the committee to use inclusive language throughout the catechism and to include the wording of the new translation of the Apostles' Creed where needed. The present edition of the Heidelberg Catechism includes these changes approved by the 1988 Synod of the CRC. Since the newly approved edition published here includes the biblical passages printed in full, it is appropriate to give special attention to the significance of biblical references in the Heidelberg Catechism.

When the first edition of the Heidelberg Catechism was published early in 1563, the German Bible had not yet been divided into verses. As a result, Scripture references in the margin of each answer included only the biblical book and chapter number. However, the Latin translation of the catechism, which appeared shortly after the first German edition, identified the precise verse or verses intended in each chapter. In the Latin translation the questions of the catechism were numbered and divided into fifty-two sections called "Lord's Days" so that a minister could preach from a different portion of the catechism each Sunday of the year. Later editions and translations of the catechism eventually included these improvements.

From the beginning, the biblical references in the Heidelberg Catechism were considered very important. Those who prepared the catechism intended it to be a faithful echo of the Scripture. Although the passages are popularly referred to as "proof texts," they are more accurately seen as "source texts." The teaching of the catechism was drawn from the Bible, and the passages listed are illustrative of the biblical sources from which each answer is drawn. Most of the biblical texts in this English translation of the catechism were included in the early

German and Latin editions, but the precise selection resulted from the CRC synodical action of 1975.

When it was first published, the Heidelberg Catechism included many more biblical references than did most catechisms of the time. Luther's Small Catechism of 1529, for example, contained very few biblical references, and these were quoted within the short answers. The catechisms of John a 'Lasco, the Polish nobleman who did so much to assist the Reformed refugee churches in England and Germany, included many biblical references. The Heidelberg Catechism followed that example. The fourth edition of November 1563 added the following explanatory note:

> The Scripture references by which the faith of the children is confirmed, are such only as have been selected with great pains from the divinely inspired Scriptures (usually called canonical books) and have been added to each question and answer.

Defenders of the Heidelberg Catechism always used biblical grounds to refute the attacks of Lutherans, Roman Catholics, and others. In 1566 Emperor Maximilian II summoned Elector Frederick III to appear before the Diet of Augsburg to face charges that his new catechism was Calvinistic in doctrine. Under the terms of the 1555 Peace of Augsburg, only Roman Catholicism and Lutheranism that was in accord with the Augsburg Confession were legally permitted in the empire. Frederick had signed the Ausburg Confession, and he stood by that signature throughout his life. Now the new catechism, his electoral office, and even his life were in danger.

Frederick courageously stated that as he prepared to appear before the Diet, he was not worried about his political office or even his own life. His chief concern was the freedom to maintain his Christian faith. In response to the charges, he declared, "So far as matters of a religious nature are involved, I confess freely that in those things which concern the conscience, I acknowledge as Master, only him, who is the Lord of lords and the King of kings . . . . The question here . . . pertains to the soul and its salvation, for which I am indebted alone to my Lord and Savior Jesus Christ, and which, as his gift, I will sacredly preserve." "Therefore," he insisted, "I cannot grant your imperial Majesty the right of standing in the place of my God and Savior."

Frederick also addressed the charge that his new catechism was Calvinistic in doctrine and therefore had no rights under the terms of the Peace of Augsburg. "What men understand by Calvinism, I do not know," he admitted. And he added, "This I can say with a pure conscience—that I have never read Calvin's writings." Frederick wanted his case to be decided simply on the basis of Scripture.

Along with several German Lutheran princes Frederick III had signed certain doctrinal statements at Frankfurt in 1558 and at Naumberg in 1561. Now, in the presence of the Emperor, he declared that he stood by that faith "on no other ground than because I find it established in the Holy Scriptures of the Old and New Testaments." He confidently added, "Nor do I believe that anyone can successfully show that I have done or received anything that stands opposed to that creed. My catechism, word for word,

is drawn, not from human, but from divine sources, the references that stand in the margin will show."

At this Diet of Augsburg Elector Frederick III stood before the powerful emperor of the Holy Roman Empire of the German nation. Some historians report that his son, John Casimir, stood at his side with an open Bible. In that dramatic setting Frederick issued this challenge:

> What I have elsewhere publicly declared to your Majesty in a full assembly of princes, namely, that if anyone of whatever age, station or class he may be, even the humblest, can teach me something better from the Holy Scriptures, I will thank him from the bottom of my heart and be readily obedient to the divine truth. This I now repeat in the presence of this assembly of the whole empire. If there be anyone here among my lords and friends who will undertake it, I am prepared to hear him, and here are the Scriptures at hand. Should it please your Imperial Majesty to undertake this task, I would regard it as the greatest favor and acknowledge it with suitable gratitude.

No one accepted the challenge! Frederick was unshaken in his biblical convictions. Yet he was enough of a realist to recognize the precariousness of his situation. "Should, contrary to my expectation, my defense and the Christian and reasonable conditions which I have proposed not be regarded of any account," he concluded, "I shall comfort myself in this: that my Lord and Savior Jesus Christ has promised to me and to all who believe that whatsoever we lose on earth for his name's sake, we shall

7

receive a hundred fold in the life to come."

Frederick's humble, yet bold and courageous defense saved the Heidelberg Catechism for the Palatinate church, and thereby for the world, throughout the rest of history. Frederick the Pious, as he came to be known after his dramatic defense, was actually a "Calvinist," even though that label meant nothing to him. Biblical faithfulness was his only concern, and that faithfulness led him to what has come to be known as "the Reformed faith," so beautifully presented in the Heidelberg Catechism.

The Christian Reformed Church publishes this edition of its new translation of the Heidelberg Catechism, including the full text of the biblical passages from the *NIV* translation of the Bible, with the hope that many will use it and that it will help to promote the kingdom of Jesus Christ.

Fred H. Klooster
December 1, 1988

LORD'S DAY 1

**1 Q. What is your only comfort
in life and in death?**

A. That I am not my own,[1]
but belong—
    body and soul,
    in life and in death—[2]
to my faithful Savior Jesus Christ.[3]

He has fully paid for all my sins with his precious blood,[4]
and has set me free from the tyranny of the devil.[5]
He also watches over me in such a way[6]
that not a hair can fall from my head
without the will of my Father in heaven:[7]
in fact, all things must work together for my salvation.[8]

Because I belong to him,
Christ, by his Holy Spirit,
assures me of eternal life[9]
and makes me wholeheartedly willing and ready
from now on to live for him.[10]

1   1 Cor. 6:19-20

Do you not know that your body is a temple of the Holy Spirit, who is in you, whom you have received from God? You are not your own; you were bought at a price. Therefore honor God with your body.

2   Rom. 14:7-9

For none of us lives to himself alone and none of us dies to himself alone. If we live, we live to the Lord; and if we die, we die to the Lord. So, whether we live or die, we belong to the Lord.

For this very reason, Christ died and returned to life so that he might be the Lord of both the dead and the living.

1 Cor. 3:23

. . . and you are of Christ, and Christ is of God.

Tit. 2:14

who gave himself for us to redeem us from all wickedness and to purify for himself a people that are his very own, eager to do what is good.

4   1 Pet. 1:18-19

For you know that it was not with perishable things such as silver or gold that you were redeemed from the empty way of life handed down to you from your forefathers, but with the precious blood of Christ, a lamb without blemish or defect.

1 John 1:7-9

But if we walk in the light, as he is in the light, we have fellowship with one another, and the blood of Jesus, his Son, purifies us from all sin.

If we claim to be without sin, we deceive ourselves and the truth is not in us. If we confess our sins, he is faithful and just and will forgive us our sins and purify us from all unrighteousness.

1 John 2:2

He is the atoning sacrifice for our sins, and not only for ours but also for the sins of the whole world.

5   John 8:34-36

Jesus replied, "I tell you the truth, everyone who sins is a slave to sin. Now a slave has no permanent place in the family, but a son belongs to it forever. So if the Son sets you free, you will be free indeed."

Heb. 2:14-15

Since the children have flesh and blood, he too shared in their humanity so that by his death he might destroy him who holds the power of death—that is, the devil—and free those who all their lives were held in slavery by their fear of death.

1 John 3:1-11

How great is the love the Father has lavished on us, that we should be called children of God! And that is what we are! The reason the world does not know us is that it did not know him. Dear friends, now we are children of God, and what we will be has not yet been made known. But we know that when he appears, we shall be like him, for we shall see him as he is. Everyone who has this hope in him purifies himself, just as he is pure.

Everyone who sins breaks the law; in fact, sin is lawlessness. But you know that he appeared so that he might take away our sins. And in him is no sin. No one who lives in him keeps on sinning. No one who continues to sin has either seen him or known him.

Dear children, do not let anyone lead you astray. He who does what is right is righteous, just as he is righteous. He who does what is sinful is of the devil, because the devil has been sinning from the beginning. The reason the Son of God appeared was to destroy the devil's work. No one who is born of God will continue to sin, because God's seed remains in him; he cannot go on sinning, because he has been born of God. This is how we know who the children of God are and who the children of the devil are: Anyone who does not do what is right is not a child of God; nor is anyone who does not love his brother.

This is the message you have heard from the beginning: We should love one another.

6   John 6:39-40

And this is the will of him who sent me, that I shall lose none of all that he has given me, but raise them up at the last day. For my Father's will is that everyone who looks to the Son and believes in him shall have eternal life, and I will raise him up at the last day.

John 10:27-30

My sheep listen to my voice; I know them, and they follow me. I give them eternal life, and they shall never perish; no one can snatch them out of my hand. My Father, who has given them to me, is greater than all; no one can snatch them out of my Father's hand. I and the Father are one.

2 Thess. 3:3

But the Lord is faithful, and he will strengthen and protect you from the evil one.

1 Pet. 1:5

who through faith are shielded by God's power until the coming of the salvation that is ready to be revealed in the last time.

7   Matt. 10:29-31

Are not two sparrows sold for a penny? Yet not one of them will fall to the ground apart from the will of your Father. And even the very hairs of your head are all numbered. So don't be afraid; you are worth more than many sparrows.

Luke 21:16-18

You will be betrayed even by parents, brothers, relatives and friends, and they will put some of you to death. All men will hate you because of me. But not a hair of your head will perish. By standing firm you will gain life.

8   Rom. 8:28

And we know that in all things God works for the good of those who love him, who have been called according to his purpose.

9   Rom. 8:15-16

For you did not receive a spirit that makes you a slave again to fear, but you received the Spirit of sonship. And by him we cry, "*Abba*, Father." The Spirit himself testifies with our spirit that we are God's children.

2 Cor. 1:21-22

Now it is God who makes both us and you stand firm in Christ. He anointed us, set his seal of ownership on us, and put his Spirit in our hearts as a deposit, guaranteeing what is to come.

2 Cor. 5:5

Now it is God who has made us for this very purpose and has given us the Spirit as a deposit, guaranteeing what is to come.

Eph. 1:13-14

And you also were included in Christ when you heard the word of truth, the gospel of your salvation. Having believed, you were marked in him with a seal, the promised Holy Spirit, who is a deposit guaranteeing our inheritance until the redemption of those who are God's possession—to the praise of his glory.

10   Rom. 8:1-17

Therefore, there is now no condemnation for those who are in Christ Jesus, because through Christ Jesus the law of the Spirit of life set me free from the law of sin and death. For what the law was powerless to do in that it was weakened by the sinful nature, God did by sending his own Son in the likeness of sinful man to be a sin offering. And so he condemned sin in sinful man, in order that the righteous requirements of the law might be fully met in us, who do not live according to the sinful nature but according to the Spirit.

Those who live according to the sinful nature have their minds set on what that nature desires;

but those who live in accordance with the Spirit have their minds set on what the Spirit desires. The mind of sinful man is death, but the mind controlled by the Spirit is life and peace; the sinful mind is hostile to God. It does not submit to God's law, nor can it do so. Those controlled by the sinful nature cannot please God.

You, however, are controlled not by the sinful nature but by the Spirit, if the Spirit of God lives in you. And if anyone does not have the Spirit of Christ, he does not belong to Christ. But if Christ is in you, your body is dead because of sin, yet your spirit is alive because of righteousness. And if the Spirit of him who raised Jesus from the dead is living in you, he who raised Christ from the dead will also give life to your mortal bodies through his Spirit, who lives in you.

Therefore, brothers, we have an obligation—but it is not to the sinful nature, to live according to it. For if you live according to the sinful nature, you will die; but if by the Spirit you put to death the misdeeds of the body, you will live, because those who are led by the Spirit of God are sons of God. For you did not receive a spirit that makes you a slave again to fear, but you received the Spirit of sonship. And by him we cry, "Abba, Father." The Spirit himself testifies with our spirit that we are God's children. Now if we are children, then we are heirs—heirs of God and co-heirs with Christ, if indeed we share in his sufferings in order that we may also share in his glory.

**2   Q. What must you know
to live and die in the joy of this comfort?**

A. Three things:
first, how great my sin and misery are;[1]
second, how I am set free from all my sins and misery;[2]
third, how I am to thank God for such deliverance.[3]

1   Rom. 3:9-10

What shall we conclude then? Are we any better? Not at all! We have already made the charge that Jews and Gentiles alike are all under sin. As it is written: "There is no one righteous, not even one . . . ."

1 John 1:10

If we claim we have not sinned, we make him out to be a liar and his word has no place in our lives.

2   John 17:3

Now this is eternal life: that they may know you, the only true God, and Jesus Christ, whom you have sent.

Acts 4:12

Salvation is found in no one else, for there is no other name under heaven given to men by which we must be saved.

Acts 10:43

All the prophets testify about him that everyone who believes in him receives forgiveness of sins through his name.

3   Matt. 5:16

In the same way, let your light shine before men, that they may see your good deeds and praise your Father in heaven.

Rom. 6:13

Do not offer the parts of your body to sin, as instruments of wickedness, but rather offer yourselves to God, as those who have been brought from death to life; and offer the parts of your body to him as instruments of righteousness.

Eph. 5:8-10

For you were once darkness, but now you are light in the Lord. Live as children of light (for the fruit of the light consists in all goodness, righteousness and truth) and find out what pleases the Lord.

2 Tim. 2:15

Do your best to present yourself to God as one approved, a workman who does not need to be ashamed and who correctly handles the words of truth.

1 Pet. 2:9-10

But you are a chosen people, a royal priesthood, a holy nation, a people belonging to God, that you may declare the praises of him who called you out of darkness into his wonderful light. Once you were not a people, but now you are the people of God; once you had not received mercy, but now you have received mercy.

LORD'S DAY 2

3   Q. **How do you come to know your misery?**

A. The law of God tells me.[1]

1   **Rom. 3:20**

Therefore no one will be declared righteous in his sight by observing the law; rather, through the law we become conscious of sin.

Rom. 7:7-25

What shall we say, then? Is the law sin? Certainly not! Indeed I would not have known what sin was except through the law. For I would not have known what coveting really was if the law had not said, "Do not covet." But sin, seizing the opportunity afforded by the commandment, produced in me every kind of covetous desire. For apart from law, sin is dead. Once I was alive apart from law; but when the commandment came, sin sprang to life and I died. I found that the very commandment that was intended to bring life actually brought death. For sin, seizing the opportunity afforded by the commandment, deceived me, and through the commandment, put me to death. So then, the law is holy, and the commandment is holy, righteous and good.

Did that which is good, then, become death to me? By no means! But in order that sin might be recognized as sin, it produced death in me through what was good, so that through the commandment sin might become utterly sinful.

We know that the law is spiritual; but I am unspiritual, sold as a slave to sin. I do not understand what I do. For what I want to do I do not do, but what I hate I do. And if I do what I do not want to do, I agree that the law is good. As it is, it is no longer I myself who do it, but it is sin living in me. I know that nothing good lives in me, that is, in my sinful nature. For I have the desire to do what is good, but I cannot carry it out. For what I do is not the good I want to do; no, the evil I do not want to do—this I keep on doing. Now if I do what I do not want to do, it is no longer I who do it, but it is sin living in me that does it.

So I find this law at work: When I want to do good, evil is right there with me. For in my inner being I delight in God's law; but I see another law at work in the members of my body, waging war against the law of my mind and making me a prisoner of the law of sin at work within my members. What a wretched man I am! Who will rescue me from this body of death? Thanks be to God—through Jesus Christ our Lord!

So then, I myself in my mind am a slave to God's law, but in the sinful nature a slave to the law of sin.

4 Q. What does God's law require of us?

A. Christ teaches us this in summary in Matthew 22—

Love the Lord your God
with all your heart
and with all your soul
and with all your mind
and with all your strength.[1]*
This is the first and greatest commandment.

And the second is like it:
Love your neighbor as yourself.[2]

All the Law and the Prophets hang
on these two commandments.

1   Deut. 6:5

Love the Lord your God with all your heart
and with all your soul and with all your strength.

2   Lev. 19:18

Do not seek revenge or bear a grudge against
one of your people, but love your neighbor as
yourself. I am the LORD.

*Earlier and better manuscripts of Matthew 22 omit the words "and with all your strength." They are found in Mark 12:30.

5 Q. Can you live up to all this perfectly?

A. No.[1]
I have a natural tendency
to hate God and my neighbor.[2]

---

1   Rom. 3:9-20, 23

What shall we conclude then? Are we any better? Not at all! We have already made the charge that Jews and Gentiles alike are all under sin. As it is written:

"There is no one righteous, not even one;
there is no one who understands,
no one who seeks God.
All have turned away,
   they have together become worthless;
there is no one who does good,
   not even one."
"Their throats are open graves;
   their tongues practice deceit."
"The poison of vipers is on their lips."
"Their mouths are full of cursing and
                bitterness."
"Their feet are swift to shed blood;
ruin and misery mark their ways,
and the way of peace they do not know."
"There is no fear of God before their eyes."

Now we know that whatever the law says, it says to those who are under the law, so that every mouth may be silenced and the whole world held accountable to God. Therefore no one will be declared righteous in his sight by observing the law; rather, through the law we become conscious of sin.
. . . For all have sinned and fall short of the glory of God.

1 John 1:8, 10

If we claim to be without sin, we deceive ourselves and the truth is not in us.
If we claim we have not sinned, we make him out to be a liar and his word has no place in our lives.

2   Gen. 6:5

The LORD saw how great man's wickedness on the earth had become, and that every inclination of the thoughts of his heart was only evil all the time.

Jer. 17:9

The heart is deceitful above all things
   and beyond cure.
Who can understand it?

Rom. 7:23-24

but I see another law at work in the members of my body, waging war against the law of my mind and making me a prisoner of the law of sin at work within my members. What a wretched man I am! Who will rescue me from this body of death?

Rom. 8:7

the sinful mind is hostile to God. It does not submit to God's law, nor can it do so.

Eph. 2:1-3

As for you, you were dead in your transgressions and sins, in which you used to live when you followed the ways of this world and of the ruler of the kingdom of the air, the spirit who is now at work in those who are disobedient. All of us also lived among them at one time, gratifying the cravings of our sinful nature and following its desires and thoughts. Like the rest, we were by nature objects of wrath.

Tit. 3:3

At one time we too were foolish, disobedient, deceived and enslaved by all kinds of passions and pleasures. We lived in malice and envy, being hated and hating one another.

6   Q. **Did God create people
so wicked and perverse?**

A. **No.**
**God created them good[1] and in his own image,[2]
that is, in true righteousness and holiness,[3]
so that they might
truly know God their creator,[4]
love him with all their heart,
and live with him in eternal happiness
for his praise and glory.[5]**

1   **Gen. 1:31**
God saw all that he had made, and it was very good. And there was evening, and there was morning—the sixth day.

2   **Gen. 1:26-27**
Then God said, "Let us make man in our image, in our likeness, and let them rule over the fish of the sea and the birds of the air, over the livestock, over all the earth, and over all the creatures that move along the ground."

So God created man in his own image,
in the image of God he created him;
male and female he created them.

3   **Eph. 4:24**
and to put on the new self, created to be like God in true righteousness and holiness.

4   **Col. 3:10**
and have put on the new self, which is being renewed in knowledge in the image of its Creator.

5   **Ps. 8**
O LORD, our Lord,
how majestic is your name in all the earth!
You have set your glory
above the heavens.
From the lips of children and infants
you have ordained praise
because of your enemies,
to silence the foe and the avenger.

When I consider your heavens,
the work of your fingers,
the moon and the stars,
which you have set in place,
what is man that you are mindful of him,
the son of man that you care for him?
You made him a little lower than the
heavenly beings
and crowned him with glory and honor.

You made him ruler over the works of
your hands;
you put everything under his feet:
all flocks and herds,
and the beasts of the field,
the birds of the air,
and the fish of the sea,
all that swim the paths of the seas.

O LORD, our Lord,
how majestic is your name in all the earth!

7 **Q. Then where does this corrupt human nature
come from?**

A. From the fall and disobedience of our first parents,
Adam and Eve, in Paradise.[1]
This fall has so poisoned our nature[2]
that we are born sinners—
corrupt from conception on.[3]

1 **Gen. 3**

Now the serpent was more crafty than any of the wild animals the LORD God had made. He said to the woman, "Did God really say, 'You must not eat from any tree in the garden'?"

The woman said to the serpent, "We may eat fruit from the trees in the garden, but God did say, 'You must not eat fruit from the tree that is in the middle of the garden, and you must not touch it, or you will die.' "

"You will not surely die," the serpent said to the woman. "For God knows that when you eat of it your eyes will be opened, and you will be like God, knowing good and evil."

When the woman saw that the fruit of the tree was good for food and pleasing to the eye, and also desirable for gaining wisdom, she took some and ate it. She also gave some to her husband, who was with her, and he ate it. Then the eyes of both of them were opened, and they realized they were naked; so they sewed fig leaves together and made coverings for themselves.

Then the man and his wife heard the sound of the LORD God as he was walking in the garden in the cool of the day, and they hid from the LORD God among the trees of the garden. But the LORD God called to the man, "Where are you?"

He answered, "I heard you in the garden, and I was afraid because I was naked; so I hid."

And he said, "Who told you that you were naked? Have you eaten from the tree that I commanded you not to eat from?"

The man said, "The woman you put here with me—she gave me some fruit from the tree, and I ate it."

Then the LORD God said to the woman, "What is this you have done?"

The woman said, "The serpent deceived me, and I ate."

So the LORD God said to the serpent,
"Because you have done this,

"Cursed are you above all the livestock
and all the wild animals!

You will crawl on your belly
and you will eat dust
all the days of your life.
And I will put enmity
between you and the woman,
and between your offspring and hers;
he will crush your head,
and you will strike his heel."

To the woman he said,

"I will greatly increase your pains in
childbearing;
with pain you will give birth to children.
Your desire will be for your husband,
and he will rule over you."

To Adam he said, "Because you listened to your wife and ate from the tree about which I commanded you, 'You must not eat of it,'

"Cursed is the ground because of you;
through painful toil you will eat of it
all the days of your life.
It will produce thorns and thistles for you,
and you will eat the plants of the field.
By the sweat of your brow
you will eat your food
until you return to the ground,
since from it you were taken;
for dust you are
and to dust you will return."

Adam named his wife Eve, because she would become the mother of all the living.

The LORD God made garments of skin for Adam and his wife and clothed them. And the LORD God said, "The man has now become like one of us, knowing good and evil. He must not be allowed to reach out his hand and take also from the tree of life and eat, and live forever." So the LORD God banished him from the Garden of Eden to work the ground from which he had been taken. After he drove the man out, he placed on the east side of the Garden of Eden cherubim and a flaming sword flashing back and forth to guard the way to the tree of life.

2   **Rom. 5:12, 18-19**

Therefore, just as sin entered the world through one man, and death through sin, and in this way death came to all men, because all sinned—

Consequently, just as the result of one trespass was condemnation for all men, so also the result of one act of righteousness was justification that brings life for all men. For just as through disobedience of the one man the many were made sinners, so also through the obedience of the one man the many will be made righteous.

3   **Ps. 51:5**

Surely I was sinful at birth,
     sinful from the time my mother conceived me.

8 **Q.** But are we so corrupt
that we are totally unable to do any good
and inclined toward all evil?

A. Yes,[1] unless we are born again,
by the Spirit of God.[2]

1 **Gen. 6:5**

The LORD saw how great man's wickedness on the earth had become, and that every inclination of the thoughts of his heart was only evil all the time.

Gen. 8:21

The LORD smelled the pleasing aroma and said in his heart: "Never again will I curse the ground because of man, even though every inclination of his heart is evil from childhood. And never again will I destroy all living creatures, as I have done."

Job 14:4

Who can bring what is pure from the impure?
No one!

Isa. 53:6

We all, like sheep, have gone astray,
each of us has turned to his own way;
and the LORD has laid on him
the iniquity of us all.

2 **John 3:3-5**

In reply Jesus declared, "I tell you the truth, no one can see the kingdom of God unless he is born again."

"How can a man be born when he is old?" Nicodemus asked. "Surely he cannot enter a second time into his mother's womb to be born!"

Jesus answered, "I tell you the truth, no one can enter the kingdom of God unless he is born of water and the Spirit."

**9 Q. But doesn't God do us an injustice
by requiring in his law
what we are unable to do?**

A. No, God created humans with the ability to keep the law.[1]
They, however, tempted by the devil,[2]
in reckless disobedience[3]
robbed themselves and all their descendants of these gifts.[4]

1 **Gen. 1:31**

God saw all that he had made, and it was very good. And there was evening, and there was morning—the sixth day.

Eph. 4:24

and to put on the new self, created to be like God in true righteousness and holiness.

2 **Gen. 3:13**

Then the LORD God said to the woman, "What is this you have done?"

The woman said, "The serpent deceived me, and I ate."

John 8:44

You belong to your father, the devil, and you want to carry out your father's desire. He was a murderer from the beginning, not holding to the truth, for there is no truth in him. When he lies, he speaks his native language, for he is a liar and the father of lies.

3 **Gen. 3:6**

When the woman saw that the fruit of the tree was good for food and pleasing to the eye, and also desirable for gaining wisdom, she took some and ate it. She also gave some to her husband, who was with her, and he ate it.

4 **Rom. 5:12, 18-19**

Therefore, just as sin entered the world through one man, and death through sin, and in this way death came to all men, because all sinned—

Consequently, just as the result of one trespass was condemnation for all men, so also the result of one act of righteousness was justification that brings life for all men. For just as through the disobedience of the one man the many were made sinners, so also through the obedience of the one man the many will be made righteous.

10 Q. Will God permit
such disobedience and rebellion
to go unpunished?

A. Certainly not.
He is terribly angry
about the sin we are born with
as well as the sins we personally commit.

As a just judge
he punishes them now and in eternity.[1]

He has declared:
"Cursed is everyone who does not continue to do
everything written in the Book of the Law."[2]

---

1   **Ex. 34:7**

maintaining love to thousands, and forgiving wickedness, rebellion and sin. Yet he does not leave the guilty unpunished; he punishes the children and their children for the sin of the fathers to the third and fourth generation.

Ps. 5:4-6

You are not a God who takes pleasure in evil;
with you the wicked cannot dwell.
The arrogant cannot stand in your presence;
you hate all who do wrong.
You destroy those who tell lies;
bloodthirsty and deceitful men
the Lord abhors.

Nah. 1:2

The Lord is a jealous and avenging God;
the Lord takes vengeance and is filled
with wrath.
The Lord takes vengeance on his foes
and maintains his wrath against his
enemies.

Rom. 1:18

The wrath of God is being revealed from heaven against all the godlessness and wickedness of men who suppress the truth by their wickedness.

Eph. 5:6

Let no one deceive you with empty words, for because of such things God's wrath comes on those who are disobedient.

Heb. 9:27

Just as man is destined to die once, and after that to face judgment,

2   **Gal. 3:10**

All who rely on observing the law are under a curse, for it is written: "Cursed is everyone who does not continue to do everything written in the Book of the Law."

Deut. 27:26

"Cursed is the man who does not uphold the words of this law by carrying them out."
Then all the people shall say, "Amen!"

21

11 Q. But isn't God also merciful?

A. God is certainly merciful,[1]
but he is also just.[2]
His justice demands
that sin, committed against his supreme majesty,
be punished with the supreme penalty—
eternal punishment of body and soul.[3]

---

1   Ex. 34:6-7

And he passed in front of Moses, proclaiming, "The LORD, the LORD, the compassionate and gracious God, slow to anger, abounding in love and faithfulness, maintaining love to thousands, and forgiving wickedness, rebellion and sin. Yet he does not leave the guilty unpunished; he punishes the children and their children for the sin of the fathers to the third and fourth generation."

Ps. 103:8-9

The LORD is compassionate and gracious,
    slow to anger, abounding in love.
He will not always accuse,
    nor will he harbor his anger forever;

2   Ex. 34:7

maintaining love to thousands, and forgiving wickedness, rebellion and sin. Yet he does not leave the guilty unpunished; he punishes the children and their children for the sin of the fathers to the third and fourth generation.

Deut. 7:9-11

Know therefore that the LORD your God is God; he is the faithful God, keeping his covenant of love to a thousand generations of those who love him and keep his commands. But
    those who hate him will repay to
        their face by destruction;
    he will not be slow to repay to their
        face those who hate him.

Therefore, take care to follow the commands, decrees and laws I give you today.

Ps. 5:4-6

You are not a God who takes pleasure in evil;
    with you the wicked cannot dwell.
The arrogant cannot stand in your presence;
    you hate all who do wrong.
You destroy those who tell lies;
    bloodthirsty and deceitful men
    the LORD abhors.

Heb. 10:30-31

For we know him who said, "It is mine to avenge; I will repay,"and again, "The Lord will judge his people." It is a dreadful thing to fall into the hands of the living God.

3   Matt. 25:35-46

" 'For I was hungry and you gave me something to eat, I was thirsty and you gave me something to drink, I was a stranger and you invited me in, I needed clothes and you clothed me, I was sick and you looked after me, I was in prison and you came to visit me.'

"Then the righteous will answer him, 'Lord, when did we see you hungry and feed you, or thirsty and give you something to drink? When did we see you a stranger and invite you in, or needing clothes and clothe you? When did we see you sick or in prison and go to visit you?'

"The King will reply, 'I tell you the truth, whatever you did for one of the least of these brothers of mine, you did for me.'

"Then he will say to those on his left, 'Depart from me, you who are cursed, into the eternal fire prepared for the devil and his angels. For I was hungry and you gave me nothing to eat, I was thirsty and you gave me nothing to drink, I was a stranger and you did not invite me in, I needed clothes and you did not clothe me, I was sick and in prison and you did not look after me.'

"They also will answer, 'Lord, when did we see you hungry or thirsty or a stranger or needing clothes or sick or in prison, and did not help you?'

"He will reply, 'I tell you the truth, whatever you did not do for one of the least of these, you did not do for me.'

"Then they will go away to eternal punishment, but the righteous to eternal life."

LORD'S DAY 5

12 Q. According to God's righteous judgment
we deserve punishment
both in this world and forever after:
how then can we escape this punishment
and return to God's favor?

A. God requires that his justice be satisfied.[1]
Therefore the claims of his justice
must be paid in full,
either by ourselves or another.[2]

1 **Ex. 23:7**

Have nothing to do with a false charge and do not put an innocent or honest person to death, for I will not acquit the guilty.

Rom. 2:1-11

You, therefore, have no excuse, you who pass judgment on someone else, for at whatever point you judge the other, you are condemning yourself, because you who pass judgment do the same things. Now we know that God's judgment against those who do such things is based on truth. So when you, a mere man, pass judgment on them and yet do the same things, do you think you will escape God's judgment? Or do you show contempt for the riches of his kindness, tolerance and patience, not realizing that God's kindness leads you toward repentance?

But because of your stubbornness and your unrepentant heart, you are storing up wrath against yourself for the day of God's wrath, when his righteous judgment will be revealed. God "will give to each person according to what he has done." To those who by persistence in doing good seek glory, honor and immortality, he will give eternal life. But for those who are self-seeking and who reject the truth and follow evil, there will be wrath and anger. There will be trouble and distress for every human being who does evil: first for the Jew, then for the Gentile; but glory, honor and peace for everyone who does good: first for the Jew, then for the Gentile. For God does not show favoritism.

2 **Isa. 53:11**

After the suffering of his soul,
    he will see the light [of life] and be satisfied;
by his knowledge my righteous servant will
        justify many,
    and he will bear their iniquities.

Rom. 8:3-4

For what the law was powerless to do in that it was weakened by the sinful nature, God did by sending his own Son in the likeness of sinful man to be a sin offering. And so he condemned sin in sinful man, in order that the righteous requirements of the law might be fully met in us, who not live according to the sinful nature but according to the Spirit.

13 Q. Can we pay this debt ourselves?

A. Certainly not.
Actually, we increase our guilt every day.[1]

1   **Matt. 6:12**

Forgive us our debts,
   as we also have forgiven our debtors.

Rom. 2:4-5

Or do you show contempt for the riches of his
kindness, tolerance and patience, not realizing
that God's kindness leads you toward repentance?
But because of your stubbornness and your
unrepentant heart, you are storing up wrath
against yourself for the day of God's wrath,
when his righteous judgment will be revealed.

**14 Q. Can another creature—any at all—
     pay this debt for us?**

A. No.
  To begin with,
    God will not punish another creature
    for what a human is guilty of.[1]
  Besides,
    no mere creature can bear the weight
    of God's eternal anger against sin
    and release others from it.[2]

1   **Ezek. 18:4, 20**

For every living soul belongs to me, the father as well as the son—both alike belong to me. The soul who sins is the one who will die.

The soul who sins is the one who will die. The son will not share the guilt of the father, nor will the father share the guilt of the son. The righteousness of the righteous man will be credited to him, and the wickedness of the wicked will be charged against him.

Heb. 2:14-18

Since the children have flesh and blood, he too shared in their humanity so that by his death he might destroy him who holds the power of death—that is, the devil—and free those who all their lives were held in slavery by their fear of death. For surely it is not angels he helps, but Abraham's descendants. For this reason he had to be made like his brothers in every way, in order that he might become a merciful and faithful high priest in service to God, and that he might make atonement for the sins of the people. Because he himself suffered when he was tempted, he is able to help those who are being tempted.

2   **Ps. 49:7-9**

No man can redeem the life of another
  or give to God a ransom for him—
the ransom for a life is costly,
  no payment is ever enough—
that he should live on forever
  and not see decay.

Ps. 130:3

If you, O LORD, kept a record of sins,
  O Lord, who could stand?

15 Q. What kind of mediator and deliverer should we look for then?

A. One who is truly human[1] and truly righteous,[2] yet more powerful than all creatures, that is, one who is also true God.[3]

[1] **Rom. 1:3**

regarding his Son, who as to his human nature was a descendant of David.

1 Cor. 15:21

For since death came through a man, the resurrection of the dead comes also through a man.

Heb. 2:17

For this reason he had to be made like his brothers in every way, in order that he might become a merciful and faithful high priest in service to God, and that he might make atonement for the sins of the people.

[2] **Isa. 53:9**

He was assigned a grave with the wicked,
and with the rich in his death,
though he had done no violence,
nor was any deceit in his mouth.

2 Cor. 5:21

God made him who had no sin to be sin for us, so that in him we might become the righteousness of God.

Heb. 7:26

Such a high priest meets our need—one who is holy, blameless, pure, set apart from sinners, exalted above the heavens.

[3] **Isa. 7:14**

Therefore the Lord himself will give you a sign: The virgin will be with child and will give birth to a son, and will call him Immanuel.

Isa. 9:6

For to us a child is born,
to us a son is given,
and the government will be on his
shoulders.
And he will be called
Wonderful Counselor, Mighty God,
Everlasting Father, Prince of Peace.

Jer. 23:6

In his days Judah will be saved
and Israel will live in safety.
This is the name by which he will be called:
The Lord Our Righteousness.

John 1:1

In the beginning was the Word, and the Word was with God, and the Word was God.

**16 Q. Why must he be truly human
and truly righteous?**

A. God's justice demands
that human nature, which has sinned,
must pay for its sin;[1]
but a sinner could never pay for others.[2]

1   **Rom. 5:12, 15**

Therefore, just as sin entered the world through one man, and death through sin, and in this way death came to all men, because all sinned—

But the gift is not like the trespass. For if the many died by the trespass of the one man, how much more did God's grace and the gift that came by the grace of the one man, Jesus Christ, overflow to the many!

1 Cor. 15:21

For since death came through a man, the resurrection of the dead comes also through a man.

Heb. 2:14-16

Since the children have flesh and blood, he too shared in their humanity so that by his death he might destroy him who holds the power of death—that is, the devil— and free those who all their lives were held in slavery by their fear of death. For surely it is not angels he helps, but Abraham's descendants.

2   **Heb. 7:26-27**

Such a high priest meets our need—one who is holy, blameless, pure, set apart from sinners, exalted above the heavens. Unlike the other high priests, he does not need to offer sacrifices day after day, first for his own sins, and then for the sins of the people. He sacrificed for their sins once for all when he offered himself.

1 Pet. 3:18

For Christ died for sins once for all, the righteous for the unrighteous, to bring you to God. He was put to death in the body but made alive by the Spirit.

17 Q. Why must he also be true God?

A. So that,
by the power of his divinity,
he might bear the weight of God's anger in his humanity
and earn for us
and restore to us
righteousness and life.[1]

Isa. 53

Who has believed our message
and to whom has the arm of the
LORD been revealed?
He grew up before him like a tender shoot,
and like a root out of dry ground.
He had no beauty or majesty to attract
us to him,
nothing in his appearance that we
should desire him.
He was despised and rejected by men,
a man of sorrows, and familiar with
suffering.
Like one from whom men hide their faces
he was despised, and we esteemed him not.

Surely he took up our infirmities
and carried our sorrows,
yet we considered him stricken by God,
smitten by him, and afflicted.
But he was pierced for our transgressions,
he was crushed for our iniquities;
the punishment that brought us
peace was upon him,
and by his wounds we are healed.
We all, like sheep, have gone astray,
each of us has turned to his own way;
and the LORD has laid on him
the iniquity of us all.

He was oppressed and afflicted,
yet he did not open his mouth;
he was led like a lamb to the slaughter,
and as a sheep before his shearers is silent,
so he did not open his mouth.
By oppression and judgment he was
taken away.
And who can speak of his descendants?
For he was cut off from the land of the
living;

for the transgression of my people
he was stricken.
He was assigned a grave with the wicked,
and with the rich in his death,
though he had done no violence,
nor was any deceit in his mouth.

Yet it was the LORD's will to crush him and
cause him to suffer,
and though the LORD makes his life a guilt
offering,
he will see his offspring and prolong his days,
and the will of the LORD will prosper
in his hand.
After the suffering of his soul,
he will see the light of life and be satisfied;
by his knowledge my righteous servant
will justify many,
and he will bear their iniquities.
Therefore I will give him a portion among
the great,
and he will divide the spoils with the strong,
because he poured out his life unto death,
and was numbered with the transgressors.
For he bore the sin of many,
and made intercession for the transgressors.

John 3:16

For God so loved the world that he gave his
one and only Son, that whoever believes in him
shall not perish but have eternal life.

2 Cor. 5:21

God made him who had no sin to be sin for
us, so that in him we might become the
righteousness of God.

18 Q. And who is this mediator—
true God and at the same time
truly human and truly righteous?

A. Our Lord Jesus Christ,[1]
who was given us
to set us completely free
and to make us right with God.[2]

1   Matt. 1:21-23

"She will give birth to a son, and you are to give him the name Jesus, because he will save his people from their sins."

All this took place to fulfill what the LORD had said through the prophet: "The virgin will be with child and will give birth to a son, and they will call him Immanuel"—which means, "God with us."

Luke 2:11

Today in the town of David a Savior has been born to you; he is Christ the Lord.

1 Tim. 2:5

For there is one God and one mediator between God and men, the man Christ Jesus.

2   1 Cor. 1:30

It is because of him that you are in Christ Jesus, who has become for us wisdom from God—that is, our righteousness, holiness and redemption.

19 Q. How do you come to know this?

    A. The holy gospel tells me.
        God himself began to reveal the gospel already in Paradise;[1]
        later, he proclaimed it
            by the holy patriarchs[2] and prophets,[3]
        and portrayed it
            by the sacrifices and other ceremonies of the law;[4]
        finally, he fulfilled it
            through his own dear Son.[5]

[1]   **Gen. 3:15**

And I will put enmity
    between you and the woman,
    and between your offspring and hers;
he will crush your head,
    and you will strike his heel.

[2]   **Gen. 22:18**

and through your offspring all nations on earth will be blessed, because you have obeyed me.

Gen. 49:10

The scepter will not depart from Judah,
    nor the ruler's staff from between his feet,
until he comes to whom it belongs
    and the obedience of the nations is his.

[3]   **Isa. 53**

See Q and A 17, footnote 1.

Jer. 23:5-6

"The days are coming," declares the LORD,
    "when I will raise up to David a
        righteous Branch,
a King who will reign wisely
    and do what is just and right in the land.
In his days Judah will be saved
    and Israel will live in safety.
This is the name by which he will be called:
    The LORD Our Righteousness."

Mic. 7:18-20

Who is a God like you,
    who pardons sin and forgives the
        transgression
of the remnant of his inheritance?
You do not stay angry forever
    but delight to show mercy.
You will again have compassion on us;
    you will tread our sins underfoot
    and hurl all our iniquities into the
        depths of the sea.
You will be true to Jacob,
    and show mercy to Abraham,
as you pledged on oath to our fathers
    in days long ago.

Acts 10:43

All the prophets testify about him that everyone who believes in him receives forgiveness of sins through his name.

Heb. 1:1-2

In the past God spoke to our forefathers through the prophets at many times and in various ways, but in these last days he has spoken to us by his Son, whom he appointed heir of all things, and through whom he made the universe.

[4]   **Lev. 1-7**

See chapters 1 through 7 of Leviticus.

John 5:46

If you believed Moses, you would believe me, for he wrote about me.

Heb. 10:1-10

The law is only a shadow of the good things that are coming—not the realities themselves. For this reason it can never, by the same sacrifices repeated endlessly year after year, make perfect those who draw near to worship. If it could, would they not have stopped being offered? For the worshipers would have been cleaned once for all, and would no longer have felt guilty for their sins. But those sacrifices are an annual reminder of sins, because it is impossible for the blood of bulls and goats to take away sins.

Therefore, when Christ came into the world, he said:
"Sacrifice and offering you did not desire,
but a body you prepared for me;
with burnt offerings and sin offerings
you were not pleased.
Then I said, 'Here I am—it is written
about me in the scroll—
I have come to do your will, O God.' "
First he said, "Sacrifices and offerings, burnt offerings and sin offerings you did not desire, nor were you pleased with them" (although the law required them to be made). Then he said, "Here I am, I have come to do your will." He sets aside the first to establish the second. And by that will, we have been made holy through the sacrifice of the body of Jesus Christ once for all.

Rom. 10:4

Christ is the end of the law so that there may be righteousness for everyone who believes.

Gal. 4:4-5

But when the time had fully come, God sent his Son, born of a woman, born under law, to redeem those under law, that we might receive the full rights of sons.

Col. 2:17

These are a shadow of the things that were to come; the reality, however, is found in Christ.

**20 Q. Are all saved through Christ
just as all were lost through Adam?**

A. No.
Only those are saved
who by true faith
are grafted into Christ
and accept all his blessings.[1]

1   **Matt. 7:14**

But small is the gate and narrow the road that leads to life, and only few find it.

John 3:16, 18, 36

For God so loved the world that he gave his one and only Son, that whoever believes in him shall not perish but have eternal life.

Whoever believes in him is not condemned, but whoever does not believe stands condemned already because he has not believed in the name of God's one and only Son.

Whoever believes in the Son has eternal life, but whoever rejects the Son will not see life, for God's wrath remains on him.

Rom. 11:16-21

If the part of the dough offered as firstfruits is holy, then the whole batch is holy; if the root is holy, so are the branches.

If some of the branches have been broken off, and you, though a wild olive shoot, have been grafted in among the others and now share in the nourishing sap from the olive root, do not boast over those branches. If you do, consider this: You do not support the root, but the root supports you. You will say then, "Branches were broken off so that I could be grafted in." Granted. But they were broken off because of unbelief, and you stand by faith. Do not be arrogant, but be afraid. For if God did not spare the natural branches, he will not spare you either.

21 Q. What is true faith?

A. True faith is
  not only a knowledge and conviction
    that everything God reveals in his Word is true;[1]
  it is also a deep-rooted assurance,[2]
    created in me by the Holy Spirit[3] through the gospel,[4]
    that, out of sheer grace earned for us by Christ,[5]
      not only others, but I too,[6]
        have had my sins forgiven,
        have been made forever right with God,
        and have been granted salvation.[7]

1 John 17:3, 17

Now this is eternal life: that they may know you, the only true God, and Jesus Christ, whom you have sent.

Sanctify them by the truth; your word is truth.

Heb. 11:1-3

Now faith is being sure of what we hope for and certain of what we do not see. This is what the ancients were commended for.

By faith we understand that the universe was formed at God's command, so that what is seen was not made out of what was visible.

James 2:19

You believe that there is one God. Good! Even the demons believe that—and shudder.

2 Rom. 4:18-21

Against all hope, Abraham in hope believed and so became the father of many nations, just as it had been said to him, "So shall your offspring be." Without weakening in his faith, he faced the fact that his body was as good as dead—since he was about a hundred years old—and that Sarah's womb was also dead. Yet he did not waver through unbelief regarding the promise of God, but was strengthened in his faith and gave glory to God, being fully persuaded that God had power to do what he had promised.

Rom. 5:1

Therefore, since we have been justified through faith, we have peace with God through our Lord Jesus Christ.

Rom. 10:10

For it is with your heart that you believe and are justified, and it is with your mouth that you confess and are saved.

Heb. 4:14-16

Therefore, since we have a great high priest who has gone through the heavens, Jesus the Son of God, let us hold firmly to the faith we profess. For we do not have a high priest who is unable to sympathize with our weakness, but we have one who has been tempted in every way, just as we are—yet was without sin. Let us then approach the throne of grace with confidence, so that we may receive mercy and find grace to help us in our time of need.

3 Matt. 16:15-17

"But what about you?" he asked. "Who do you say I am?"

Simon Peter answered, "You are the Christ, the Son of the living God."

Jesus replied, "Blessed are you, Simon son of Jonah, for this was not revealed to you by man, but by my Father in heaven."

John 3:5

Jesus answered, "I tell you the truth, no one can enter the kingdom of God unless he is born of water and the Spirit."

Acts 16:14

One of those listening was a woman named Lydia, a dealer in purple cloth from the city of Thyatira, who was a worshiper of God. The Lord opened her heart to respond to Paul's message.

4 Rom. 1:16

I am not ashamed of the gospel, because it is the power of God for the salvation of everyone who believes: first for the Jew, then for the Gentile.

Rom. 10:17

Consequently, faith comes from hearing the message, and the message is heard through the word of Christ.

1 Cor. 1:21

For since in the wisdom of God the world through its wisdom did not know him, God was pleased through the foolishness of what was preached to save those who believe.

5 ### Rom. 3:21-26

But now a righteousness from God, apart from law, has been made known, to which the law and the Prophets testify. This righteousness from God comes through faith in Jesus Christ to all who believe. There is no difference, for all have sinned and fall short of the glory of God, and are justified freely by his grace through the redemption that came by Christ Jesus. God presented him as a sacrifice of atonement, through faith in his blood. He did this to demonstrate his justice, because in his forbearance he had left the sins committed beforehand unpunished—he did it to demonstrate his justice at the present time, so as to be just and the one who justifies those who have faith in Jesus.

Gal. 2:16

know that a man is not justified by observing the law, but by faith in Jesus Christ. So we, too, have put our faith in Christ Jesus that we may be justified by faith in Christ and not by observing the law, because by observing the law no one will be justified.

Eph. 2:8-10

For it is by grace you have been saved, through faith—and this not from yourselves, it is the gift of God—not by works, so that no one can boast. For we are God's workmanship, created in Christ Jesus to do good works, which God prepared in advance for us to do.

6 ### Gal. 2:20

I have been crucified with Christ and I no longer live, but Christ lives in me. The life I live in the body, I live by faith in the Son of God, who loved me and gave himself for me.

7 ### Rom. 1:17

For in the gospel a righteousness from God is revealed, a righteousness that is by faith from first to last, just as it is written: "The righteous will live by faith."

Heb. 10:10

And by that will, we have been made holy through the sacrifice of the body of Jesus Christ once for all.

22 Q. What then must a Christian believe?

A. Everything God promises us in the gospel.[1]
   That gospel is summarized for us
   in the articles of our Christian faith—
   a creed beyond doubt,
   and confessed throughout the world.

---

[1] **Matt. 28:18-20**

Then Jesus came to them and said, "All authority in heaven and on earth has been given to me. Therefore go and make disciples of all nations, baptizing them in the name of the Father and of the Son and of the Holy Spirit, and teaching them to obey everything I have commanded you. And surely I am with you always, to the very end of the age."

John 20:30-31

Jesus did many other miraculous signs in the presence of his disciples, which are not recorded in this book. But these are written that you may believe that Jesus is the Christ, the Son of God, and that by believing you may have life in his name.

23 Q. What are these articles?

A. I believe in God, the Father almighty,
    creator of heaven and earth.

I believe in Jesus Christ, his only Son, our Lord,
    who was conceived by the Holy Spirit
    and born of the Virgin Mary.
    He suffered under Pontius Pilate,
    was crucified, died, and was buried;
    he descended to hell.
    The third day he rose again from the dead.
    He ascended to heaven
    and is seated at the right hand of God the Father almighty.
    From there he will come to judge the living and the dead.

I believe in the Holy Spirit,
    the holy catholic church,
    the communion of saints,
    the forgiveness of sins,
    the resurrection of the body,
    and the life everlasting. Amen.

24 Q. How are these articles divided?

 A. Into three parts:
    God the Father and our creation;
    God the Son and our deliverance;
    God the Holy Spirit and our sanctification.

25 Q. Since there is but one God,[1]
why do you speak of three:
Father, Son, and Holy Spirit?

A. Because that is how
God has revealed himself in his Word:[2]
these three distinct persons
are one true, eternal God.

[1] **Deut. 6:4**

Hear, O Israel: The Lord our God, the Lord is one.

1 Cor. 8:4, 6

So then, about eating food sacrificed to idols: We know that an idol is nothing at all in the world and that there is no God but one.

yet for us there is but one God, the Father, from whom all things came and for whom we live; and there is but one Lord, Jesus Christ, through whom all things came and through whom we live.

[2] **Matt. 3:16-17**

As soon as Jesus was baptized, he went up out of the water. At that moment heaven was opened, and he saw the Spirit of God descending like a dove and lighting on him. And a voice from heaven said, "This is my Son, whom I love; with him I am well pleased."

Matt. 28:18-19

Then Jesus came to them and said, "All authority in heaven and on earth has been given to me. Therefore go and make disciples of all nations, baptizing them in the name of the Father and of the Son and of the Holy Spirit . . . ."

Luke 4:18 (Isa. 61:1)

The Spirit of the Lord is on me,
because he has anointed me
to preach good news to the poor.
He has sent me to proclaim freedom for
the prisoners
and recovery of sight for the blind,
to release the oppressed . . . .

John 14:26

But the counselor, the Holy Spirit, whom the Father will send in my name, will teach you all things and will remind you of everything I have said to you.

John 15:26

When the Counselor comes, whom I will send to you from the Father, the Spirit of truth who goes out from the Father, he will testify about me.

2 Cor. 13:14

May the grace of the Lord Jesus Christ, and the love of God, and the fellowship of the Holy Spirit be with you all.

Gal. 4:6

Because you are sons, God sent the Spirit of his Son into our hearts, the Spirit who calls out, *"Abba*, Father."

Tit. 3:5-6

he saved us, not because of righteous things we had done, but because of his mercy. He saved us through the washing of rebirth and renewal by the Holy Spirit, whom he poured out on us generously through Jesus Christ our Savior . . . .

God the Father

**26 Q. What do you believe when you say,
"I believe in God, the Father almighty,
creator of heaven and earth"?**

A. That the eternal Father of our Lord Jesus Christ,
  who out of nothing created heaven and earth
    and everything in them,[1]
  who still upholds and rules them
    by his eternal counsel and providence,[2]
is my God and Father
  because of Christ his Son.[3]

I trust him so much that I do not doubt
  he will provide
    whatever I need
    for body and soul,[4]
  and he will turn to my good
    whatever adversity he sends me
    in this sad world.[5]

He is able to do this because he is almighty God;[6]
he desires to do this because he is a faithful Father.[7]

---

1   **Gen. 1 and 2**

In the beginning God created the heavens and the earth. Now the earth was formless and empty, darkness was over the surface of the deep, and the Spirit of God was hovering over the waters.

And God said, "Let there be light," and there was light. God saw that the light was good, and he separated the light from the darkness. God called the light "day," and the darkness he called "night." And there was evening, and there was morning—the first day.

And God said, "Let there be an expanse between the waters to separate water from water." So God made the expanse and separated the water under the expanse from the water above it. And it was so. God called the expanse "sky." And there was evening, and there was morning—the second day.

And God said, "Let the water under the sky be gathered to one place, and let dry ground appear." And it was so. God called the dry ground "land," and the gathered waters he called "seas." And God saw that it was good.

Then God said, "Let the land produce vegetation: seed-bearing plants and trees on the land that bear fruit with seed in it, according to their various kinds." And it was so. The land produced vegetation: plants bearing seed according to their kinds and trees bearing fruit with seed in it according to their kinds. And God saw that it was good. And there was evening, and there was morning—the third day.

And God said, "Let there be lights in the expanse of the sky to separate the day from the night, and let them serve as signs to mark seasons and days and years, and let them be lights in the expanse of the sky to give light on the earth." And it was so. God made two great lights—the greater light to govern the day and the lesser light to govern the night. He also made the stars. God sent them in the expanse of the sky to give light on the earth, to govern the day and the night, and to separate light from darkness. And God saw that it was good. And there was evening, and there was morning—the fourth day.

And God said, "Let the water teem with living creatures, and let birds fly above the earth across the expanse of the sky." So God created the great creatures of the sea and every living and moving thing with which the water teems, according to their kinds, and every winged bird according to its kind. And God saw that it was good. God blessed them and said, "Be fruitful and increase in number and fill the water in the seas, and let the birds increase on the earth." And there was evening, and there was morning—the fifth day.

And God said, "Let the land produce living creatures according to their kinds: livestock, creatures that move along the ground, and wild animals, each according to its kind." And it was so. God made the wild animals according to their kinds, the livestock according to their kinds, and all the creatures that move along the ground according to their kinds. And God saw that it was good.

Then God said, "Let us make man in our image, in our likeness, and let them rule over the fish of the sea and the birds of the air, over the livestock, over all the earth, and over all the creatures that move along the ground."

So God created man in his own image,
in the image of God, he created him;
male and female, he created them.

God blessed them and said to them, "Be fruitful and increase in number; fill the earth and subdue it. Rule over the fish of the sea and the birds of the air and over every living creature that moves on the ground."

Then God said, "I give you every seed-bearing plant on the face of the whole earth and every tree that has fruit with seed in it. They will be yours for food. And to all the beasts of the earth and all the birds of the air and all the creatures that move on the ground—everything that has the breath of life in it—I give every green plant for food." And it was so.

God saw all that he had made, and it was very good. And there was evening, and there was morning—the sixth day.

Thus the heavens and the earth were completed in all their vast array.

By the seventh day God had finished the work he had been doing; so on the seventh day he rested from all his work. And God blessed the seventh day and made it holy, because on it he rested from all the work of creating that he had done.

This is the account of the heavens and the earth when they were created.

When the LORD God made the earth and the heavens—and no shrub of the field had yet appeared on the earth and no plant of the field had yet sprung up, for the LORD God had not sent rain on the earth, and there was no man to work the ground, but streams came up from the earth and watered the whole surface of the ground—the LORD God formed the man from the dust of the ground and breathed into his nostrils the breath of life, and the man became a living being.

Now the LORD God had planted a garden in the east, in Eden; and there he put the man he had formed. And the LORD God made all kinds of trees grow out of the ground—trees that were pleasing to the eye and good for food. In the middle of the garden were the tree of life and the tree of the knowledge of good and evil.

A river watering the garden flowed from Eden; from there it was separated into four headwaters. The name of the first is the Pishon; it winds through the entire land of Havilah, where there is gold. (The gold of that land is good; aromatic resin and onyx are also there.) The name of the second river is the Gihon; it winds through the entire land of Cush. The name of the third river is the Tigris; it runs along the east side of Asshur. And the fourth river is the Euphrates.

The LORD God took the man and put him in the Garden of Eden to work it and take care of it. And the LORD God commanded the man, "You are free to eat from any tree in the garden; but you must not eat from the tree of the knowledge of good and evil, for when you eat of it you will surely die."

The LORD God said, "It is not good for the man to be alone. I will make a helper suitable for him."

Now the LORD God had formed out of the ground all the beasts of the field and all the birds of the air. He brought them to the man to see what he would name them; and whatever the man called each living creature, that was its name. So the man gave names to all the livestock, the birds of the air and all the beasts of the field.

But for Adam no suitable helper was found. So the LORD God caused the man to fall into a deep sleep; and while he was sleeping, he took one of the man's ribs and closed up the place with flesh. Then the LORD God made a woman from the rib he had taken out of the man, and he brought her to the man.

The man said,

"This is now bone of my bones
    and flesh of my flesh;
she shall be called 'woman,'
    for she was taken out of man."

For this reason a man will leave his father and mother and be united to his wife, and they will become one flesh.

The man and his wife were both naked, and they felt no shame.

Ex. 20:11

For in six days the Lord made the heavens and the earth, the sea, and all that is in them, but he rested on the seventh day. Therefore the Lord blessed the Sabbath day and made it holy.

Ps. 33:6

By the word of the Lord were the heavens made, their starry host by the breath of his mouth.

Isa. 44:24

This is what the Lord says—
your Redeemer, who formed you
in the womb:

I am the Lord,
who has made all things,
who alone stretched out the heavens,
who spread out the earth by myself . . . .

Acts 4:24

When they heard this, they raised their voice together in prayer to God. "Sovereign Lord," they said, "you made the heaven and the earth and the sea, and everything in them."

Acts 14:15

Men, why are you doing this? We too are only men, human like you. We are bringing you good news, telling you to turn from these worthless things to the living God, who made heaven and earth and sea and everything in them.

2 Ps. 104

Praise the Lord, O my soul.

O Lord my God, you are very great;
 you are clothed with splendor and majesty.
He wraps himself in light as with a garment;
 he stretches out the heavens like a tent
and lays the beams of his upper
   chambers on their waters.
He makes the clouds his chariot
 and rides on the wings of the wind.
He makes winds his messengers,
 flames of fire his servants.

He set the earth on its foundations;
 it can never be moved.
You covered it with the deep as with a garment;
 the waters stood above the mountains.
But at your rebuke the waters fled,
 at the sound of your thunder they
   took to flight;
they flowed over the mountains,
 they went down into the valleys,
 to the place you assigned for them.
You set a boundary they cannot cross;
 never again will they cover the earth.
He makes springs pour water into the ravines;
 it flows between the mountains.
They give water to all the beasts of the field;
 the wild donkeys quench their thirst.

The birds of the air nest by the waters;
 they sing among the branches.
He waters the mountains from his
   upper chambers;
 the earth is satisfied by the fruit of his work.
He makes grass grow for the cattle,
 and plants for man to cultivate—
 bringing forth food from the earth:
wine that gladdens the heart of man,
 oil to make his face shine,
 and bread that sustains his heart.
The trees of the Lord are well watered,
 the cedars of Lebanon that he planted.
There the birds make their nests;
 the stork has its home in the pine trees.
The high mountains belong to the wild goats;
 the crags are a refuge for the coneys.

The moon marks off the seasons,
 and the sun knows when to go down.
You bring darkness, it becomes night,
 and all the beasts of the forest prowl.
The lions roar for their prey
 and seek their food from God.
The sun rises, and they steal away;
 they return and lie down in their dens.
Then man goes out to his work,
 to his labor until evening.

How many are your works, O Lord!
 In wisdom you made them all;
 the earth is full of your creatures.
There is the sea, vast and spacious,
 teeming with creatures beyond number—
 living things both large and small.
There the ships go to and fro,
and the leviathan, which you
   formed to frolic there.

These all look to you
 to give them their food at the proper time.
When you give it to them,
 they gather it up;
when you open your hand,
 they are satisfied with good things.
When you hide your face,
 they are terrified;
when you take away their breath,
 they die and return to the dust.
When you send your Spirit,
 they are created,
and you renew the face of the earth.

May the glory of the Lord endure forever;
 may the Lord rejoice in his works—
he who looks at the earth, and it trembles,
 who touches the mountains, and
   they smoke.

I will sing to the Lord all my life;
 I will sing praise to my God as long as I live.
May my meditation be pleasing to him,
 as I rejoice in the Lord.

But may sinners vanish from the earth
and the wicked be no more.

Praise the Lord, O my soul.

Praise the Lord.

Matt. 6:30

If that is how God clothes the grass of the field,
which is here today and tomorrow is thrown
into the fire, will he not much more clothe you,
O you of little faith?

Matt. 10:29

Are not two sparrows sold for a penny? Yet not
one of them will fall to the ground apart from
the will of your Father.

Eph. 1:11

In him we were also chosen, having been predestined according to the plan of him who works
out everything in conformity with the purpose
of his will.

3   John 1:12-13

Yet to all who received him, to those who
believed in his name, he gave the right to become children of God—children born not of
natural descent, nor of human decision or a
husband's will, but born of God.

Rom. 8:15-16

For you did not receive a spirit that makes
you a slave again to fear, but you received the
Spirit of sonship. And by him we cry "*Abba*,
Father." The Spirit himself testifies with our
spirit that we are God's children.

Gal. 4:4-7

But when the time had fully come, God sent
his Son, born of a woman, born under law, to
redeem those under law, that we might receive
the full rights of sons. Because you are sons, God
sent the Spirit of his Son into our hearts, the
Spirit who calls out, "*Abba*, Father." So you are
no longer a slave, but a son; and since you are a
son, God has made you also an heir.

Eph. 1:5

He predestined us to be adopted as his sons
through Jesus Christ, in accordance with his
pleasure and will—

4   Ps. 55:22

Cast your cares on the Lord
and he will sustain you;
he will never let the righteous fall.

Matt. 6:25-26

Therefore I tell you, do not worry about your
life, what you will eat or drink; or about your
body, what you will wear. Is not life more important than food, and the body more important
than clothes? Look at the birds of the air; they do
not sow or reap or store away in barns, and yet
your heavenly Father feeds them. Are you not
much more valuable than they?

Luke 12:22-31

Then Jesus said to his disciples: "Therefore I
tell you, do not worry about your life, what you
will eat; or about your body, what you will wear.
Life is more than food, and the body more than
clothes. Consider the ravens: They do not sow or
reap, they have no storeroom or barn; yet God
feeds them. And how much more valuable you
are than birds! Who of you by worrying can add
a single hour to his life? Since you cannot do this
very little thing, why do you worry about the
rest?

"Consider how the lilies grow. They do not
labor or spin. Yet I tell you, not even Solomon in
all his splendor was dressed like one of these. If
that is how God clothes the grass of the field,
which is here today, and tomorrow is thrown
into the fire, how much more will he clothe you,
O you of little faith! And do not set your heart on
what you will eat or drink; do not worry about
it. For the pagan world runs after all such things,
and your Father knows that you need them. But
seek his kingdom, and these things will be given
to you as well."

5   Rom. 8:28

And we know that in all things God works for
the good of those who love him, who have been
called according to his purpose.

6   Gen. 18:14

Is anything too hard for the Lord? I will return
to you at the appointed time next year and Sarah
will have a son.

What, then, shall we say in response to this? If God is for us, who can be against us? He who did not spare his own Son, but gave him up for us all—how will he not also, along with him, graciously give us all things? Who will bring any charge against those whom God has chosen? It is God who justifies. Who is he that condemns? Christ Jesus, who died—more than that, who was raised to life—is at the right hand of God and is also interceding for us. Who shall separate us from the love of Christ? Shall trouble or hardship or persecution or famine or nakedness or danger or sword? As it is written:

"For your sake we face death all day long;
we are considered as sheep to be
slaughtered."

No, in all these things we are more than conquerors through him who loved us. For I am convinced that neither death nor life, neither angels nor demons, neither the present nor the future, nor any powers, neither height nor depth, nor anything else in all creation, will be able to separate us from the love of God that is in Christ Jesus our Lord.

Which of you, if his son asks for bread, will give him a stone? Or if he asks for a fish, will give him a snake? If you, then, though you are evil, know how to give good gifts to your children, how much more will your Father in heaven give good gifts to those who ask him!

27 **Q.** **What do you understand**
by the providence of God?

A. Providence is
the almighty and ever present power of God[1]
by which he upholds, as with his hand,
heaven
and earth
and all creatures[2]
and so rules them that
leaf and blade,
rain and drought,
fruitful and lean years,
food and drink,
health and sickness,
prosperity and poverty—[3]
all things, in fact, come to us
not by chance[4]
but from his fatherly hand.[5]

[1]   Jer. 23:23-24

"Am I only a God nearby,"
declares the LORD,
"and not a God far away?
Can anyone hide in secret places
so that I cannot see him?"
declares the LORD.
"Do not I fill heaven and earth?"
declares the LORD.

Acts 17:24-28

"The God who made the world and everything in it is the Lord of heaven and earth and does not live in temples built by hands. And he is not served by human hands, as if he needed anything, because he himself gives all men life and breath and everything else. From one man he made every nation of men, that they should inhabit the whole earth; and he determined the times set for them and the exact places where they should live. God did this so that men would seek him and perhaps reach out for him and find him, though he is not far from each one of us. 'For in him we live and move and have our being.' As some of your own poets have said, 'We are his offspring.' "

[2]   Heb. 1:3

The Son is the radiance of God's glory and the exact representation of his being, sustaining all things by his powerful word. After he had provided purification for sins, he sat down at the right hand of the Majesty in heaven.

[3]   Jer. 5:24

They do not say to themselves,
"Let us fear the LORD our God,
who gives autumn and spring rains in season,
who assures us of the regular weeks
of harvest."

Acts 14:15-17

Men, why are you doing this? We too are only men, human like you. We are bringing you good news, telling you to turn from these worthless things to the living God, who made heaven and earth and sea and everything in them. In the past, he let all nations go their own way. Yet he has not left himself without testimony: He has shown kindness by giving you rain from heaven and crops in their seasons: he provides you with plenty of food and fills your hearts with joy.

John 9:3

"Neither this man nor his parents sinned," said Jesus, "but this happened so that the work of God might be displayed in his life."

Prov. 22:2

Rich and poor have this in common:
The LORD is the Maker of them all.

4   **Prov. 16:33**

The lot is cast into the lap,
    but its every decision is from the Lord.

5   **Matt. 10:29**

Are not two sparrows sold for a penny? Yet not one of them will fall to the ground apart from the will of your Father.

28 Q. **How does the knowledge
of God's creation and providence
help us?**

A. **We can be patient when things go against us,[1]
thankful when things go well,[2]
and for the future we can have
good confidence in our faithful God and Father
that nothing will separate us from his love.[3]
All creatures are so completely in his hand
that without his will
they can neither move nor be moved.[4]**

1   Job 1:21-22
and said:
"Naked I came from my mother's womb,
    and naked I will depart.
The Lord gave and the Lord has taken away;
    may the name of the Lord be praised."
In all this, Job did not sin by charging God
with wrongdoing.

James 1:3
. . . because you know that the testing of your
faith develops perseverance.

2   Deut. 8:10
When you have eaten and are satisfied, praise
the Lord your God for the good land he has
given you.

1 Thess. 5:18
give thanks in all circumstances, for this is
God's will for you in Christ Jesus.

3   Ps. 55:22
Cast your cares on the Lord
    and he will sustain you;
    he will never let the righteous fall.

Rom. 5:3-5
Not only so, but we also rejoice in our suffering, because we know that suffering produces
perseverance; perseverance, character; and character, hope. And hope does not disappoint us, because God has poured out his love into our
hearts by the Holy Spirit, whom he has given us.

Rom. 8:38-39
For I am convinced that neither death nor life,
neither angels nor demons, neither the present
nor the future, nor any powers, neither height
nor depth, nor anything else in all creation, will
be able to separate us from the love of God that
is in Christ Jesus our Lord.

4   Job 1:12
The Lord said to Satan, "Very well, then, every-
thing he has is in your hands, but on the man
himself do not lay a finger."
Then Satan went out from the presence of the
Lord.

Job 2:6
The Lord said to Satan, "Very well, then, he is
in your hands; but you must spare his life."

Prov. 21:1
The king's heart is in the hand of the Lord;
    he directs it like a watercourse
        wherever he pleases.

Acts 17:24-28
"The God who made the world and everything in it is the Lord of heaven and earth and
does not live in temples built by hands. And he
is not served by human hands, as if he needed
anything, because he himself gives all men life
and breath and everything else. From one man
he made every nation of men, that they should
inhabit the whole earth; and he determined the
times set for them and the exact places where
they should live. God did this so that men would
seek him and perhaps reach out for him and find
him, though he is not far from each one of us.
'For in him we live and move and have our
being.' As some of your own poets have said,
'We are his offspring.' "

LORD'S DAY 11

29 Q. Why is the Son of God called "Jesus,"
meaning "savior"?

A. Because he saves us from our sins.[1]
Salvation cannot be found in anyone else;
it is futile to look for any salvation elsewhere.[2]

1 **Matt. 1:21**

She will give birth to a son, and you are to give him the name Jesus, because he will save his people from their sins.

Heb. 7:25

Therefore he is able to save completely those who come to God through him, because he always lives to intercede for them.

2 **Isa. 43:11**

I, even I, am the LORD,
and apart from me there is no savior.

John 15:5

I am the vine; you are the branches. If a man remains in me and I in him, he will bear much fruit; apart from me you can do nothing.

Acts 4:11-12

He is
" 'the stone you builders rejected,
which has become the capstone.'

Salvation is found in no one else, for there is no other name under heaven given to men by which we must be saved."

1 Tim. 2:5

For there is one God and one mediator between God and men, the man Christ Jesus . . . .

30 Q. Do those who look for
       their salvation and security
       in saints, in themselves, or elsewhere
       really believe in the only savior Jesus?

    A. No.
       Although they boast of being his,
       by their deeds they deny
       the only savior and deliverer, Jesus.[1]

       Either Jesus is not a perfect savior,
       or those who in true faith accept this savior
       have in him all they need for their salvation.[2]

[1] **1 Cor. 1:12-13**

What I mean is this: One of you says, "I follow Paul"; another, "I follow Apollos"; another, "I follow Cephas"; still another, "I follow Christ." Is Christ divided? Was Paul crucified for you? Were you baptized into the name of Paul?

Gal. 5:4

You who are trying to be justified by law have been alienated from Christ; you have fallen away from grace.

[2] **Col. 1:19-20**

For God was pleased to have all his fullness dwell in him, and through him to reconcile to himself all things, whether things on earth or things in heaven, by making peace through his blood, shed on the cross.

Col. 2:10

and you have been given fullness in Christ, who is the head over every power and authority.

1 John 1:7

But if we walk in the light, as he is in the light, we have fellowship with one another, and the blood of Jesus, his Son, purifies us from all sin.

31 Q. Why is he called "Christ,"
meaning "anointed"?

A. Because he has been ordained by God the Father
and has been anointed with the Holy Spirit[1]
to be
our chief prophet and teacher[2]
who perfectly reveals to us
the secret counsel and will of God for our deliverance;[3]
our only high priest[4]
who has set us free by the one sacrifice of his body,[5]
and who continually pleads our cause with the Father;[6]
and our eternal king[7]
who governs us by his Word and Spirit,
and who guards us and keeps us
in the freedom he has won for us.[8]

---

1   **Luke 3:21-22**

When all the people were being baptized, Jesus was baptized too. And as he was praying, heaven was opened and the Holy Spirit descended on him in bodily form like a dove. And a voice came from heaven: "You are my Son, whom I love; with you I am well pleased."

Luke 4:14-19 (Isa. 61:1)

Jesus returned to Galilee in the power of the Spirit, and news about him spread through the whole countryside. He taught in their synagogues, and everyone praised him.

He went to Nazareth, where he had been brought up, and on the Sabbath day he went into the synagogue, as was his custom. And he stood up to read. The scroll of the prophet Isaiah was handed to him. Unrolling it, he found the place where it is written:

"The Spirit of the Lord is on me,
  because he has anointed me
  to preach good news to the poor.
He has sent me to proclaim freedom for
    the prisoners
  and recovery of sight for the blind,
to release the oppressed,
  to proclaim the year of the Lord's favor."

Heb. 1:9 (Ps. 45:7)

You have loved righteousness and hated
    wickedness;
  therefore God, your God, has set you
    above your companions
by anointing you with the oil of
    joy.

2   **Acts 3:22 (Deut. 18:15)**

For Moses said, "The Lord your God will raise up for you a prophet like me from among your own people; you must listen to everything he tells you."

3   **John 1:18**

No one has ever seen God, but God the One and Only, who is at the Father's side, has made him known.

John 15:15

I no longer call you servants, because a servant does not know his master's business. Instead, I have called you friends, for everything that I learned from my Father I have made known to you.

4   **Heb. 7:17 (Ps. 110:4)**

For it is declared:

"You are a priest forever,
  in the order of Melchizedek."

5   **Heb. 9:12**

He did not enter by means of the blood of goats and calves; but he entered the Most Holy Place once for all by his own blood, having obtained eternal redemption.

Heb. 10:11-14

Day after day every priest stands and performs his religious duties; again and again he offers the same sacrifices, which can never take away sins. But when this priest had offered for all time one sacrifice for sins, he sat down at the right hand of God. Since that time he waits for his enemies to be made his footstool, because by one sacrifice he has made perfect forever those who are being made holy.

6   Rom. 8:34

Who is he that condemns? Christ Jesus, who died—more than that, who was raised to life—is at the right hand of God and is also interceding for us.

Heb. 9:24

For Christ did not enter a man-made sanctuary that was only a copy of the true one; he entered heaven itself, now to appear for us in God's presence.

7   Matt. 21:5 (Zech. 9:9)

"Say to the Daughter of Zion,
  'See, your king comes to you,
gentle and riding on a donkey,
  on a colt, the foal of a donkey.' "

8   Matt. 28:18-20

Then Jesus came to them and said, "All authority in heaven and on earth has been given to me. Therefore go and make disciples of all nations, baptizing them in the name of the Father and of the Son and of the Holy Spirit, and teaching them to obey everything I have commanded you. And surely I am with you always, to the very end of the age."

John 10:28

I give them eternal life, and they shall never perish; no one can snatch them out of my hand.

Rev. 12:10-11

Then I heard a loud voice in heaven say:

"Now have come the salvation and
      the power and the kingdom of
      our God,
  and the authority of his Christ.
For the accuser of our brothers,
    who accuses them before our God
      day and night,
  has been hurled down.
They overcame him
  by the blood of the Lamb
  and by the word of their testimony;
they did not love their lives so much
  as to shrink from death."

32 Q. But why are you called a Christian?

A. Because by faith I am a member of Christ[1]
and so I share in his anointing.[2]

I am anointed
to confess his name,[3]
to present myself to him as a living sacrifice of thanks,[4]
to strive with a good conscience against sin and the devil
in this life,[5]
and afterward to reign with Christ
over all creation
for all eternity.[6]

1 **1 Cor. 12:12-27**

The body is a unit, though it is made up of many parts; and though all its parts are many, they form one body. So it is with Christ. For we were all baptized by one Spirit into one body—whether Jews or Greeks, slave or free—and we were all given the one Spirit to drink.

Now the body is not made up of one part but of many. If the foot should say, "Because I am not a hand, I do not belong to the body," it would not for that reason cease to be part of the body. And if the ear should say, "Because I am not an eye, I do not belong to the body," it would not for that reason cease to be part of the body. If the whole body were an eye, where would the sense of hearing be? If the whole body were an ear, where would the sense of smell be? But in fact God has arranged the parts in the body, every one of them, just as he wanted them to be. If they were all one part, where would the body be? As it is, there are many parts, but one body.

The eye cannot say to the hand, "I don't need you!" And the head cannot say to the feet, "I don't need you!" On the contrary, those parts of the body that seem to be weaker are indispensable, and the parts that we think are less honorable we treat with special honor. And the parts that are unpresentable are treated with special modesty, while our presentable parts need no special treatment. But God has combined the members of the body and has given greater honor to the parts that lacked it, so that there should be no division in the body, but that its parts should have equal concern for each other. If one part suffers, every part suffers with it; if one part is honored, every part rejoices with it.

Now you are the body of Christ and each one of you is a part of it.

2 **Acts 2:17 (Joel 2:28)**

In the last days, God says,
I will pour out my Spirit on all people.
Your sons and daughters will prophecy,
your young men will see visions,
your old men will dream dreams.

1 John 2:27

As for you, the anointing you received from him remains in you, and you do not need anyone to teach you. But as his anointing teaches you about all things and as that anointing is real, not counterfeit—just as it has taught you, remain in him.

3 **Matt. 10:32**

Whoever acknowledges me before men, I will also acknowledge him before my Father in heaven.

Rom. 10:9-10

That if you confess with your mouth, "Jesus is Lord," and believe in your heart that God raised him from the dead, you will be saved. For it is with your heart that you believe and are justified, and it is with your mouth that you confess and are saved.

Heb. 13:15

Through Jesus, therefore, let us continually offer to God a sacrifice of praise—the fruit of lips that confess his name.

4 **Rom. 12:1**

Therefore, I urge you, brothers, in view of God's mercy, to offer your bodies as living sacrifices, holy and pleasing to God—this is your spiritual act of worship.

1 Pet. 2:5, 9

you also, like living stones, are being built into a spiritual house to be a holy priesthood, offering spiritual sacrifices acceptable to God through Jesus Christ.

But you are a chosen people, a royal priesthood, a holy nation, a people belonging to God, that you may declare the praises of him who called you out of darkness into his wonderful light.

51

5   Gal. 5:16-17

So I say, live by the Spirit, and you will not gratify the desires of the sinful nature. For the sinful nature desires what is contrary to the Spirit, and the Spirit what is contrary to the sinful nature. They are in conflict with each other, so that you do not do what you want.

Eph. 6:11

Put on the full armor of God so that you can take your stand against the devil's schemes.

1 Tim. 1:18-19

Timothy, my son, I give you this instruction in keeping with the prophecies once made about you, so that by following them you may fight the good fight, holding on to faith and a good conscience. Some have rejected these and so have shipwrecked their faith.

6   Matt. 25:34

"Then the King will say to those on his right, 'Come, you who are blessed by my Father; take your inheritance, the kingdom prepared for you since the creation of the world.' "

2 Tim. 2:12

if we endure,
 we will also reign with him.
If we disown him,
 he will also disown us . . . .

**33 Q. Why is he called God's "only Son"
when we also are God's children?**

**A. Because Christ alone is the eternal, natural Son of God.[1]
We, however, are adopted children of God—
adopted by grace through Christ.[2]**

1   **John 1:1-3, 14, 18**

In the beginning was the Word, and the Word was with God, and the Word was God. He was with God in the beginning.

Through him all things were made; without him nothing was made that has been made.

The Word became flesh and made his dwelling among us. We have seen his glory, the glory of the One and Only, who came from the Father, full of grace and truth.

No one has ever seen God, but God the One and Only, who is at the Father's side, has made him known.

Heb. 1

In the past God spoke to our forefathers through the prophets at many times and in various ways, but in these last days he has spoken to us by his Son, whom he appointed heir of all things, and through whom he made the universe. The Son is the radiance of God's glory and the exact representation of his being, sustaining all things by his powerful word. After he had provided purification for sins, he sat down at the right hand of the Majesty in heaven. So he became as much superior to the angels as the name he has inherited is superior to theirs.

For to which of the angels did God ever say,

"You are my Son;
today I have become your Father"?

Or again,

"I will be his Father,
and he will be my Son"?

And again, when God brings his firstborn into the world, he says,

"Let all God's angels worship him."

In speaking of the angels he says,

"He makes his angels winds,
his servants flames of fire."

But about the Son he says,

"Your throne, O God, will last for ever and ever,
and righteousness will be the scepter
of your kingdom.

You have loved righteousness and hated
wickedness;
therefore God, your God, has set you
above your companions
by anointing you with the oil of joy."

He also says,

"In the beginning, O Lord, you laid the
foundations of the earth,
and the heavens are the work of your hands.
They will perish, but you remain;
they will all wear out like a garment.
You will roll them up like a robe;
like a garment they will be changed.
But you remain the same,
and your years will never end."

To which of the angels did God ever say,

"Sit at my right hand
until I make your enemies
a footstool for your feet"?

Are not all angels ministering spirits sent to serve those who will inherit salvation?

2   **John 1:12**

Yet to all who received him, to those who believed in his name, he gave the right to become children of God—

Rom. 8:14-17

because those who are led by the Spirit of God are sons of God. For you did not receive a spirit that makes you a slave again to fear, but you received the Spirit of sonship. And by him we cry, "*Abba*, Father." The Spirit himself testifies with our spirit that we are God's children. Now if we are children, then we are heirs—heirs of God and co-heirs with Christ, if indeed we share in his suffering in order that we may also share in his glory.

Eph. 1:5-6

he predestined us to be adopted as his sons through Jesus Christ, in accordance with his pleasure and will—to the praise of his glorious grace, which he has freely given us in the One he loves.

34 Q. Why do you call him "our Lord"?

    A. Because—
            not with gold or silver,
            but with his precious blood—[1]
        he has set us free
            from sin and from the tyranny of the devil,[2]
        and has bought us,
            body and soul,
        to be his very own.[3]

[1]   **1 Pet. 1:18-19**

For you know that it was not with perishable things such as silver or gold that you were redeemed from the empty way of life handed down to you from your forefathers, but with the precious blood of Christ, a lamb without blemish or defect.

[2]   **Col. 1:13-14**

For he has rescued us from the dominion of darkness and brought us into the kingdom of the Son he loves, in whom we have redemption, the forgiveness of sins.

Heb. 2:14-15

Since the children have flesh and blood, he too shared in their humanity so that by his death he might destroy him who holds the power of death—that is, the devil—and free those who all their lives were held in slavery by their fear of death.

[3]   **1 Cor. 6:20**

you were bought at a price. Therefore honor God with your body.

1 Tim. 2:5-6

For there is one God and one mediator between God and men, the man Christ Jesus, who gave himself as a ransom for all men—the testimony given in its proper time.

**35 Q. What does it mean that he
"was conceived by the Holy Spirit
and born of the Virgin Mary"?**

A. That the eternal Son of God,
who is and remains
true and eternal God,[1]
took to himself,
through the working of the Holy Spirit,[2]
from the flesh and blood of the Virgin Mary,[3]
a truly human nature
so that he might become David's true descendant,[4]
like his brothers in every way[5]
except for sin.[6]

1   **John 1:1**

In the beginning was the Word, and the Word was with God, and the Word was God.

John 10:30-36

"I and the Father are one."

Again the Jews picked up stones to stone him, but Jesus said to them, "I have shown you many great miracles from the Father. For which of these do you stone me?"

"We are not stoning you for any of these," replied the Jews, "but for blasphemy, because you, a mere man, claim to be God."

Jesus answered them, "Is it not written in your Law, 'I have said you are gods'? If he called them 'gods,' to whom the word of God came—and the Scripture cannot be broken—what about the one whom the Father set apart as his very own and sent into the world? Why then do you accuse me of blasphemy because I said, 'I am God's Son'?"

Acts 13:33 (Ps. 2:7)

he has fulfilled for us, their children, by raising up Jesus. As it is written in the second Psalm:
" 'You are my Son;
today I have become your Father.' "

Col. 1:15-17

He is the image of the invisible God, the firstborn over all creation. For by him all things were created: things in heaven and on earth, visible and invisible, whether thrones or powers or rulers or authorities; all things were created by him and for him. He is before all things, and in him all things hold together.

1 John 5:20

We know also that the Son of God has come and has given us understanding, so that we may know him who is true. And we are in him who is true—even in his Son Jesus Christ. He is the true God and eternal life.

2   Luke 1:35

The angel answered, "The Holy Spirit will come upon you, and the power of the Most High will overshadow you. So the holy one to be born will be called the Son of God."

3   Matt. 1:18-23

This is how the birth of Jesus Christ came about: His mother Mary was pledged to be married to Joseph, but before they came together, she was found to be with child through the Holy Spirit. Because Joseph her husband was a righteous man and did not want to expose her to public disgrace, he had in mind to divorce her quietly.

But after he had considered this, an angel of the Lord appeared to him in a dream and said, "Joseph son of David, do not be afraid to take Mary home as your wife, because what is conceived in her is from the Holy Spirit. She will give birth to a son, and you are to give him the name Jesus, because he will save his people from their sins."

All this took place to fulfill what the Lord had said through the prophet: "The virgin will be with child and will give birth to a son, and they will call him Immanuel"—which means, "God with us."

John 1:14

The Word became flesh and made his dwelling among us. We have seen his glory, the glory of the One and Only, who came from the Father, full of grace and truth.

Gal. 4:4

But when the time had fully come, God sent his Son, born of a woman, born under law . . .

Heb. 2:14

Since the children have flesh and blood, he too shared in their humanity so that by his death he might destroy him who holds the power of death—that is, the devil . . . .

4
2 Samuel 7:12-16

When your days are over and you rest with your fathers, I will raise up your offspring to succeed you, who will come from your own body, and I will establish his kingdom. He is the one who will build a house for my Name, and I will establish the throne of his kingdom forever. I will be his father, and he will be my son. When he does wrong, I will punish him with the rod of men, with floggings inflicted by men. But my love will never be taken away from him, as I took it away from Saul, whom I removed from before you. Your house and your kingdom will endure forever before me; your throne will be established forever.

Psalm 132:11

The Lord swore an oath to David,
a sure oath that he will not revoke:
"One of your own descendants
I will place on your throne—"

Matthew 1:1

A record of the genealogy of Jesus Christ the son of David, the son of Abraham:

Romans 1:3

regarding his Son, who as to his human nature was a descendant of David.

5
Phil. 2:7

but made himself nothing,
taking the very nature of a servant,
being made in human likeness.

Heb. 2:17

For this reason he had to be made like his brothers in every way, in order that he might become a merciful and faithful high priest in service to God, and that he might make atonement for the sins of the people.

6
Heb. 4:15

For we do not have a high preist who is unable to sympathize with our weaknesses, but we have one who has been tempted in every way, just as we are—yet was without sin.

Heb. 7:26-27

Such a high priest meets our need—one who is holy, blameless, pure, set apart from sinners, exalted above the heavens. Unlike the other high priests, he does not need to offer sacrifices day after day, first for his own sins, and then for the sins of the people. He sacrificed for their sins once for all when he offered himself.

36 Q. How does the holy conception and birth of Christ benefit you?

A. He is our mediator,[1]
and with his innocence and perfect holiness
he removes from God's sight
my sin—mine since I was conceived.[2]

1   **1 Tim. 2:5-6**

For there is one God and one mediator between God and men, the man Christ Jesus, who gave himself as a ransom for all men—the testimony given it its proper time.

Heb. 9:13-15

The blood of goats and bulls and the ashes of a heifer sprinkled on those who are ceremonially unclean sanctify them so that they are outwardly clean. How much more, then, will the blood of Christ, who through the eternal Spirit offered himself unblemished to God, cleanse our consciences from acts that lead to death, so that we may serve the living God!

For this reason Christ is the mediator of a new covenant, that those who are called may receive the promised eternal inheritance—now that he has died as a ransom to set them free from the sins committed under the first covenant.

2   **Rom. 8:3-4**

For what the law was powerless to do in that it was weakened by the sinful nature, God did by sending his own Son in the likeness of sinful man to be a sin offering. And so he condemned sin in sinful man, in order that the righteous requirements of the law might be fully met in us, who do not live according to the sinful nature but according to the Spirit.

2 Cor. 5:21

God made him who had no sin to be sin for us, so that in him, we might become the righteousness of God.

Gal. 4:4-5

But when the time had fully come, God sent his Son, born of a woman, born under law, to redeem those under law, that we might receive the full rights of sons.

1 Pet. 1:18-19

For you know that it was not with perishable things such as silver or gold that you were redeemed from the empty way of life handed down to you from your forefathers, but with the precious blood of Christ, a lamb without blemish or defect.

37 **Q.** **What do you understand
by the word "suffered"?**

A. That during his whole life on earth,
but especially at the end,
Christ sustained
in body and soul
the anger of God against the sin of the whole human race.[1]

This he did in order that,
by his suffering as the only atoning sacrifice,[2]
he might set us free, body and soul,
from eternal condemnation,[3]
and gain for us
God's grace,
righteousness,
and eternal life.[4]

[1] **Isa. 53**

Who has believed our message
and to whom has the arm of the
LORD been revealed?
He grew up before him like a tender shoot,
and like a root out of dry ground.
He had no beauty or majesty to attract
us to him,
nothing in his appearance that we
should desire him.
He was despised and rejected by men,
a man of sorrows, and familiar with
suffering.
Like one from whom men hide their faces
he was despised, and we esteemed him not.

Surely he took up our infirmities
and carried our sorrows,
yet we considered him stricken by God,
smitten by him, and afflicted.
But he was pierced for our transgressions,
he was crushed for our iniquities;
the punishment that brought us
peace was upon him,
and by his wounds we are healed.
We all, like sheep, have gone astray,
each of us has turned to his own way;
and the LORD has laid on him
the iniquity of us all.

He was oppressed and afflicted,
yet he did not open his mouth;
he was led like a lamb to the slaughter,
and as a sheep before his shearers is silent,
so he did not open his mouth.

By oppression and judgment he was
taken away.
And who can speak of his descendants?
For he was cut off from the land of the
living;
for the transgression of my people
he was stricken.
He was assigned a grave with the wicked,
and with the rich in his death,
though he had done no violence,
nor was any deceit in his mouth.

Yet it was the LORD's will to crush
him and cause him to suffer,
and though the LORD makes his life
a guilt offering,
he will see his offspring and prolong his days,
and the will of the LORD will
prosper in his hand.
After the suffering of his soul,
he will see the light of life and be satisfied;
by his knowledge my righteous
servant will justify many,
and he will bear their iniquities.
Therefore I will give him a portion
among the great,
and he will divide the spoils with the strong,
because he poured out his life unto death,
and was numbered with the transgressors.
For he bore the sin of many,
and made intercession for the transgressors.

1 Pet. 2:24

He himself bore our sins in his body on the tree, so that we might die to sins and live for righteousness; by his wounds you have been healed.

1 Pet. 3:18

For Christ died for sins once for all, the righteous for the unrighteous, to bring you to God. He was put to death in the body but made alive by the Spirit . . . .

2   Rom. 3:25

God presented him as a sacrifice of atonement, through faith in his blood. He did this to demonstrate his justice, because in his forbearance he had left the sins committed beforehand unpunished—

Heb. 10:14

because by one sacrifice he has made perfect forever those who are being made holy.

1 John 2:2

He is the atoning sacrifice for our sins, and not only for ours but also for the sins of the whole world.

1 John 4:10

This is love: not that we loved God, but that he loved us and send his Son as an atoning sacrifice for our sins.

3   Rom. 8:1-4

Therefore, there is now no condemnation for those who are in Christ Jesus, because through Christ Jesus the law of the Spirit of life set me free from the law of sin and death. For what the law was powerless to do in that it was weakened by the sinful nature, God did by sending his own Son in the likeness of sinful man to be a sin offering. And so he condemned sin in sinful man, in order that the righteous requirements of the law might be fully met in us, who do not live according to the sinful nature but according to the Spirit.

Gal. 3:13

Christ redeemed us from the curse of the law by becoming a curse for us, for it is written: "Cursed is everyone who is hung on a tree."

4   John 3:16

For God so loved the world that he gave his one and only Son, that whosoever believes in him shall not perish but have eternal life.

Rom. 3:24-26

and are justified freely by his grace through the redemption that came by Christ Jesus. God presented him as a sacrifice of atonement, through faith in his blood. He did this to demonstrate his justice, because in his forbearance he had left the sins committed beforehand unpunished—he did it to demonstrate his justice at the present time, so as to be just and the one who justifies those who have faith in Jesus.

**38 Q. Why did he suffer
"under Pontius Pilate" as judge?**

A. So that he,
though innocent,
might be condemned by a civil judge,[1]
and so free us from the severe judgment of God
that was to fall on us.[2]

[1]   Luke 23:13-24

Pilate called together the chief priests, the rulers and the people, and said to them, "You brought me this man as one who was inciting the people to rebellion. I have examined him in your presence and have found no basis for your charges against him. Neither had Herod, for he sent him back to us; as you can see, he has done nothing to deserve death. Therefore, I will punish him and then release him."

With one voice they cried out, "Away with this man! Release Barabbas to us!" (Barabbas had been thrown into prison for an insurrection in the city, and for murder.)

Wanting to release Jesus, Pilate appealed to them again. But they kept shouting, "Crucify him! Crucify him!"

For the third time he spoke to them: "Why? What crime has this man committed? I have found in him no grounds for the death penalty. Therefore I will have him punished and then release him."

But with loud shouts they insistently demanded that he be crucified, and their shouts prevailed. So Pilate decided to grant their demand.

John 19:4, 12-16

Once more Pilate came out and said to the Jews, "Look, I am bringing him out to you to let you know that I find no basis for a charge against him."

From then on, Pilate tried to set Jesus free, but the Jews kept shouting, "If you let this man go, you are no friend of Caesar. Anyone who claims to be a king opposes Caesar."

When Pilate heard this, he brought Jesus out and sat down on the judge's seat at a place known as the Stone Pavement (which in Aramaic is Gabbatha). It was the day of Preparation of Passover Week, about the sixth hour.

"Here is your king," Pilate said to the Jews.

But they shouted, "Take him away! Take him away! Crucify him!"

"Shall I crucify your king?" Pilate asked.

"We have no king but Caesar," the chief priests answered.

Finally Pilate handed him over to them to be crucified.

[2]   Isa. 53:4-5

Surely he took up our infirmities
and carried our sorrows,
yet we considered him stricken by God,
smitten by him, and afflicted.
But he was pierced for our transgressions,
he was crushed for our iniquities;
the punishment that brought us
peace was upon him,
and by his wounds we are healed.

2 Cor. 5:21

God made him who had no sin to be sin for us, so that in him we might become the righteousness of God.

Gal. 3:13

Christ redeemed us from the curse of the law by becoming a curse for us, for it is written: "Cursed is everyone who is hung on a tree."

39 Q. Is it significant
      that he was "crucified"
      instead of dying some other way?

    A. Yes.
      This death convinces me
      that he shouldered the curse
      which lay on me,
      since death by crucifixion was accursed by God.[1]

---

1   Gen. 3:10-13 (Deut. 21:23)

All who rely on observing the law are under a curse, for it is written: "Cursed is everyone who does not continue to do everything written in the Book of the Law." Clearly no one is justified before God by the law, because, "The righteous will live by faith." The law is not based on faith; on the contrary, "The man who does these things will live by them." Christ redeemed us from the curse of the law by becoming a curse for us, for it is written: "Cursed is everyone who is hung on a tree."

40 Q. Why did Christ have to go all the way to death?

A. Because God's justice and truth demand it:[1]
only the death of God's Son could pay for our sin.[2]

---

1 Gen. 2:17

but you must not eat from the tree of the knowledge of good and evil, for when you eat of it you will surely die.

2 Rom. 8:3-4

For what the law was powerless to do in that it was weakened by the sinful nature, God did by sending his own Son in the likeness of sinful man to be a sin offering. And so he condemned sin in sinful man, in order that the righteous requirements of the law might be fully met in us, who do not live according to the sinful nature but according to the Spirit.

Phil. 2:8

And being found in appearance as a man,
he humbled himself
and became obedient to death—
even death on a cross!

Heb. 2:9

But we see Jesus, who was made a little lower than the angels, now crowned with glory and honor because he suffered death, so that by the grace of God he might taste death for everyone.

41 Q. Why was he "buried"?

A. His burial testifies
that he really died.[1]

[1]
Isa. 53:9
He was assigned a grave with the wicked,
    and with the rich in his death,
though he had done no violence,
    nor was any deceit in his mouth.

John 19:38-42
Later, Joseph of Arimathea asked Pilate for the body of Jesus. Now Joseph was a disciple of Jesus, but secretly because he feared the Jews. With Pilate's permission, he came and took the body away. He was accompanied by Nicodemus, the man who earlier had visited Jesus at night. Nicodemus brought a mixture of myrrh and aloes, about seventy-five pounds. Taking Jesus' body, the two of them wrapped it, with the spices, in strips of linen. This was in accordance with Jewish burial customs. At the place where Jesus was crucified, there was a garden, and in the garden a new tomb, in which no one had ever been laid. Because it was the Jewish day of Preparation and since the tomb was nearby, they laid Jesus there.

Acts 13:29
When they had carried out all that was written about him, they took him down from the tree and laid him in a tomb.

1 Cor. 15:3-4
For what I received I passed on to you as of first importance: that Christ died for our sins according to the Scriptures, that he was buried, that he was raised on the third day according to the Scriptures . . . .

**42 Q. Since Christ has died for us,
why do we still have to die?**

A. Our death does not pay the debt of our sins.[1]
Rather, it puts an end to our sinning
and is our entrance into eternal life.[2]

1   **Ps. 49:7**

No man can redeem the life of another
or give to God a ransom for him—

2   **John 5:24**

I tell you the truth, whoever hears my word
and believes him who sent me has eternal life
and will not be condemned; he has crossed over
from death to life.

Phil. 1:21-23

For to me, to live is Christ and to die is gain. If
I am to go on living in the body, this will mean
fruitful labor for me. Yet what shall I choose? I
do not know! I am torn between the two: I desire
to depart and be with Christ, which is better by
far . . . .

1 Thess. 5:9-10

For God did not appoint us to suffer wrath
but to receive salvation through our Lord Jesus
Christ. He died for us so that, whether we are
awake or asleep, we may live together with him.

**43 Q. What further advantage do we receive
from Christ's sacrifice and death on the cross?**

A. Through Christ's death
our old selves are crucified, put to death, and buried with him,[1]
so that the evil desires of the flesh
may no longer rule us,[2]
but that instead we may dedicate ourselves
as an offering of gratitude to him.[3]

1   **Rom. 6:5-11**

If we have been united with him like this in his death, we will certainly also be united with him in his resurrection. For we know that our old self was crucified with him so that the body of sin might be done away with, that we should no longer be slaves to sin— because anyone who has died has been freed from sin.

Now if we died with Christ, we believe that we will also live with him. For we know that since Christ was raised from the dead, he cannot die again; death no longer has mastery over him. The death he died, he died to sin once for all; but the life he lives, he lives to God.

In the same way, count yourselves dead to sin but alive to God in Christ Jesus.

Col. 2:11-12

In him you were also circumcised, in the putting off of the sinful nature, not with a circumcision done by the hands of men but with the circumcision done by Christ, having been buried with him in baptism and raised with him through your faith in the power of God, who raised him from the dead.

2   **Rom. 6:12-14**

Therefore do not let sin reign in your mortal body so that you obey its evil desires. Do not offer the parts of your body to sin, as instruments of wickedness, but rather offer yourselves to God, as those who have been brought from death to life; and offer the parts of your body to him as instruments of righteousness. For sin shall not be your master, because you are not under law, but under grace.

3   **Rom. 12:1**

Therefore, I urge you, brothers, in view of God's mercy, to offer your bodies as living sacrifices, holy and pleasing to God—this is your spiritual act of worship.

Eph. 5:1-2

Be imitators of God, therefore, as dearly loved children and live a life of love, just as Christ loved us and gave himself up for us as a fragrant offering and sacrifice to God.

**44 Q. Why does the creed add,
"He descended to hell"?**

A. To assure me in times of personal crisis and temptation
   that Christ my Lord,
   by suffering unspeakable anguish, pain, and terror of soul,
   especially on the cross but also earlier,
   has delivered me from the anguish and torment of hell.[1]

1   Isa. 53

Who has believed our message
and to whom has the arm of the
   LORD been revealed?
He grew up before him like a tender shoot,
   and like a root out of dry ground.
He had no beauty or majesty to attract
   us to him,
nothing in his appearance that we
   should desire him.
He was despised and rejected by men,
   a man of sorrows, and familiar with
   suffering.
Like one from whom men hide their faces
   he was despised, and we esteemed him not.

Surely he took up our infirmities
   and carried our sorrows,
yet we considered him stricken by God,
   smitten by him, and afflicted.
But he was pierced for our transgressions,
   he was crushed for our iniquities;
the punishment that brought us
   peace was upon him,
   and by his wounds we are healed.
We all, like sheep, have gone astray,
   each of us has turned to his own way;
and the LORD has laid on him
   the iniquity of us all.

He was oppressed and afflicted,
   yet he did not open his mouth;
he was led like a lamb to the slaughter,
   and as a sheep before his shearers is silent,
   so he did not open his mouth.
By oppression and judgment he was
   taken away.
And who can speak of his descendants?
For he was cut off from the land of the
   living;
for the transgression of my people
   he was stricken.
He was assigned a grave with the wicked,
   and with the rich in his death,
though he had done no violence,
   nor was any deceit in his mouth.

Yet it was the LORD's will to crush
   him and cause him to suffer,
and though the LORD makes his life
   a guilt offering,
he will see his offspring and prolong his days,

and the will of the LORD will
   prosper in his hand.
After the suffering of his soul,
   he will see the light of life and be satisfied;
by his knowledge my righteous
   servant will justify many,
   and he will bear their iniquities.
Therefore I will give him a portion
   among the great,
   and he will divide the spoils with the strong,
because he poured out his life unto death,
   and was numbered with the transgressors.
For he bore the sin of many,
   and made intercession for the transgressors.

Matt. 26:36-46

Then Jesus went with his disciples to a place
called Gethsemane, and he said to them, "Sit
here while I go over there and pray." He took
Peter and the two sons of Zebedee along with
him, and he began to be sorrowful and troubled.
Then he said to them, "My soul is overwhelmed
with sorrow to the point of death. Stay here and
keep watch with me."
   Going a little farther, he fell with his face to
the ground and prayed, "My Father, if it is possible, may this cup be taken from me. Yet not as I
will, but as you will."
   Then he returned to his disciples and found
them sleeping. "Could you men not keep watch
with me for one hour?" he asked Peter. "Watch
and pray so that you will not fall into temptation. The spirit is willing, but the body is weak."
   He went away a second time and prayed,
"My Father, if it is not possible for this cup to be
taken away unless I drink it, may your will be
done."
   When he came back, he again found them
sleeping, because their eyes were heavy. So he
left them and went away once more and prayed
the third time, saying the same thing.
   Then he returned to the disciples and said to
them, "Are you still sleeping and resting? Look,
the hour is near, and the Son of Man is betrayed
into the hands of sinners. Rise, let us go! Here
comes my betrayer!"

Matt. 27:45-46

From the sixth hour until the ninth hour darkness came over all the land. About the ninth hour Jesus cried out in a loud voice, *"Eloi, Eloi, lama sabachthani?"*—which means, "My God, my God, why have you forsaken me?"

Luke 22:44

And being in anguish, he prayed more earnestly, and his sweat was like drops of blood falling to the ground.

Heb. 5:7-10

During the days of Jesus' life on earth, he offered up prayers and petitions with loud cries and tears to the one who could save him from death, and he was heard because of his reverent submission. Although he was a son, he learned obedience from what he suffered and, once made perfect, he became the source of eternal salvation for all who obey him and was designated by God to be high priest in the order of Melchizedek.

45 Q. How does Christ's resurrection benefit us?

A. First, by his resurrection he has overcome death,
so that he might make us share in the righteousness
he won for us by his death.[1]

Second, by his power we too
are already now resurrected to a new life.[2]

Third, Christ's resurrection
is a guarantee of our glorious resurrection.[3]

1　　　　Rom. 4:25

He was delivered over to death for our sins and was raised to life for our justification.

1 Cor. 15:16-20

For if the dead are not raised, then Christ has not been raised either. And if Christ has not been raised, your faith is futile; you are still in your sins. Then those also who have fallen asleep in Christ are lost. If only for this life we have hope in Christ, we are to be pitied more than all men.

But Christ has indeed been raised from the dead, the firstfruits of those who have fallen asleep. For since death came through a man, the resurrection of the dead comes also through a man.

1 Pet. 1:3-5

Praise be to the God and Father of our Lord Jesus Christ. In his great mercy he has given us new birth into a living hope through the resurrection of Jesus Christ from the dead, and into an inheritance that can never perish, spoil or fade—kept in heaven for you, who through faith are shielded by God's power until the coming of the salvation that is ready to be revealed in the last time.

2　　　　Rom. 6:5-11

If we have been united with him like this in his death, we will certainly also be united with him in his resurrection. For we know that our old self was crucified with him so that the body of sin might be done away with, that we should no longer be slaves to sin—because anyone who has died has been freed from sin.

Now if we died with Christ, we believe that we will also live with him. For we know that since Christ was raised from the dead, he cannot die again; death no longer has mastery over him. The death he died, he died to sin once for all; but the life he lives, he lives to God.

In the same way, count yourselves dead to sin but alive to God in Christ Jesus.

Eph. 2:4-6

But because of his great love for us, God, who is rich in mercy, made us alive with Christ even when we were dead in transgressions—it is by grace you have been saved. And God raised us up with Christ and seated us with him in the heavenly realms in Christ Jesus . . . .

Col. 3:1-4

Since, then, you have been raised with Christ, set your hearts on things above, where Christ is seated at the right hand of God. Set your minds on things above, not on earthly things. For you died, and your life is now hidden with Christ in God. When Christ, who is your life, appears, then you also will appear with him in glory.

Phil. 3:20-21

But our citizenship is in heaven. And we eagerly await a Savior from there, the Lord Jesus Christ, who, by the power that enables him to bring everything under his control, will transform our lowly bodies so that they will be like his glorious body.

3

Rom. 8:11

And if the Spirit of him who raised Jesus from the dead is living in you, he who raised Christ from the dead will also give life to your mortal bodies through his Spirit, who lives in you.

1 Cor. 15:12-23

But if it is preached that Christ has been raised from the dead, how can some of you say that there is no resurrection of the dead? If there is no resurrection of the dead, then not even Christ has been raised. And if Christ has not been raised, our preaching is useless and so is your faith. More than that, we are then found to be false witnesses about God, for we have testified about God that he raised Christ from the dead. But he did not raise him if in fact the dead are not raised. For if the dead are not raised, then Christ has not been raised either. And if Christ has not been raised, your faith is futile; you are still in your sins. Then those also who have fallen asleep in Christ are lost. If only for this life we have hope in Christ, we are to be pitied more than all men.

But Christ has indeed been raised from the dead, the firstfruits of those who have fallen asleep. For since death came through a man, the resurrection of the dead comes also through a man. For as in Adam all die, so in Christ all will be made alive. But each in his own turn: Christ, the firstfruits; then, when he comes, those who belong to him.

**46 Q. What do you mean by saying,
"He ascended to heaven"?**

A. That Christ,
while his disciples watched,
was lifted up from the earth to heaven[1]
and will be there for our good[2]
until he comes again
to judge the living and the dead.[3]

1   Luke 24:50-51

When he had led them out to the vicinity of Bethany, he lifted up his hands and blessed them. While he was blessing them, he left them and was taken up into heaven.

Acts 1:9-11

After he said this, he was taken up before their very eyes, and a cloud hid him from their sight.

They were looking intently up into the sky as he was going, when suddenly two men dressed in white stood beside them. "Men of Galilee," they said, "why do you stand here looking into the sky? This same Jesus, who has been taken from you into heaven, will come back in the same way you have seen him go into heaven."

2   Rom. 8:34

Who is he that condemns? Christ Jesus, who died—more than that, who was raised to life—is at the right hand of God and is also interceding for us.

Eph. 4:8-10

This is why it says:

"When he ascended on high,
he led captives in his train
and gave gifts to men."

(What does "he ascended" mean except that he also descended to the lower, earthly regions? He who descended is the very one who ascended higher than all the heavens, in order to fill the whole universe.)

Heb. 7:23-25

Now there have been many of those priests, since death prevented them from continuing in office; but because Jesus lives forever, he has a permanent priesthood. Therefore he is able to save completely those who come to God through him, because he always lives to intercede for them.

Heb. 9:24

For Christ did not enter a man-made sanctuary that was only a copy of the true one; he entered heaven itself, now to appear for us in God's presence.

3   Acts 1:11

"Men of Galilee," they said, "why do you stand here looking into the sky? This same Jesus, who has been taken from you into heaven, will come back in the same way you have seen him go into heaven."

47 Q. But isn't Christ with us
 until the end of the world
 as he promised us?[1]

 A. Christ is truly human and truly God.
 In his human nature Christ is not now on earth;[2]
 but in his divinity, majesty, grace, and Spirit
 he is not absent from us for a moment.[3]

---

1   **Matt. 28:20**

and teaching them to obey everything I have commanded you. And surely I am with you always, to the very end of the age.

2   **Acts 1:9-11**

After he said this, he was taken up before their very eyes, and a cloud hid him from their sight.

They were looking intently up into the sky as he was going, when suddenly two men dressed in white stood beside them. "Men of Galilee," they said, "why do you stand here looking into the sky? This same Jesus, who has been taken from you into heaven, will come back in the same way you have seen him go into heaven."

Acts 3:19-21

Repent, then, and turn to God, so that your sins may be wiped out, that times of refreshing may come from the Lord, and that he may send the Christ, who has been appointed for you— even Jesus. He must remain in heaven until the time comes for God to restore everything, as he promised long ago through his holy prophets.

3   **Matt. 28:18-20**

Then Jesus came to them and said, "All authority in heaven and on earth has been given to me. Therefore go and make disciples of all nations, baptizing them in the name of the Father and of the Son and of the Holy Spirit, and teaching them to obey everything I have commanded you. And surely I am with you always, to the very end of the age."

John 14:16-19

And I will ask the Father, and he will give you another Counselor to be with you forever—the Spirit of truth. The world cannot accept him, because it neither sees him nor knows him. But you know him, for he lives with you and will be in you. I will not leave you as orphans; I will come to you. Before long, the world will not see me anymore, but you will see me. Because I live, you also will live.

48 Q. **If his humanity is not present**
wherever his divinity is,
then aren't the two natures of Christ
separated from each other?

A. Certainly not.
Since divinity
is not limited
and is present everywhere,[1]
it is evident that
Christ's divinity is surely beyond the bounds of
the humanity he has taken on,
but at the same time his divinity is in
and remains personally united to
his humanity.[2]

[1]   **Jer. 23:23-24**
"Am I only a God nearby,"
             declares the LORD,
"and not a God far away?
Can anyone hide in secret places
so that I cannot see him?"
             declares the LORD.
"Do not I fill heaven and earth?"
             declares the LORD.

Acts 7:48-49 (Isa. 66:1)
"However, the Most High does not live in
houses made by men. As the prophet says:

" 'Heaven is my throne,
and the earth is my footstool.
What kind of house will you build for me?
says the Lord.
Or where will my resting place be?' "

[2]   **John 1:14**
The Word became flesh and made his dwelling among us. We have seen his glory, the glory of the One and Only, whom came from the Father, full of grace and truth.

John 3:13
No one has ever gone into heaven except the one who came from heaven—the Son of Man.

Col. 2:9
For in Christ all the fullness of the Deity lives in bodily form . . . .

49 Q. How does Christ's ascension to heaven benefit us?

A. First, he pleads our cause
    in heaven
    in the presence of his Father.[1]

Second, we have our own flesh in heaven—
    a guarantee that Christ our head
    will take us, his members,
    to himself in heaven.[2]

Third, he sends his Spirit to us on earth
    as a further guarantee.[3]
By the Spirit's power
    we make the goal of our lives,
      not earthly things,
    but the things above where Christ is,
      sitting at God's right hand.[4]

---

[1]   **Rom. 8:34**

Who is he that condemns? Christ Jesus, who died—more than that, who was raised to life—is at the right hand of God and is also interceding for us.

1 John 2:1

My dear children, I write this to you so that you will not sin. But if anybody does sin, we have one who speaks to the Father in our defense—Jesus Christ, the Righteous One.

[2]   **John 14:2**

In my Father's house are many rooms; if it were not so, I would have told you. I am going there to prepare a place for you.

John 17:24

Father, I want those you have given me to be with me where I am, and to see my glory, the glory you have given me because you loved me before the creation of the world.

Eph. 2:4-6

But because of his great love for us, God, who is rich in mercy, made us alive with Christ even when we were dead in transgressions—it is by grace you have been saved. And God raised us up with Christ and seated us with him in the heavenly realms in Christ Jesus.

[3]   **John 14:16**

And I will ask the Father, and he will give you another Counselor to be with your forever—

2 Cor. 1:21-22

Now it is God who makes both us and you stand firm in Christ. He anointed us, set his seal of ownership on us, and put his Spirit in our hearts as a deposit, guaranteeing what is to come.

2 Cor. 5:5

Now it is God who has made us for this very purpose and has given us the Spirit as a deposit, guaranteeing what is to come.

[4]   **Col. 3:1-4**

Since, then, you have been raised with Christ, set your hearts on things above, where Christ is seated at the right hand of God. Set your minds on things above, not on earthly things. For you died, and your life is now hidden with Christ in God. When Christ, who is your life, appears, then you also will appear with him in glory.

50 Q. Why the next words:
"and is seated at the right hand of God"?

A. Christ ascended to heaven,
there to show that he is head of his church,[1]
and that the Father rules all things through him.[2]

---

1 Eph. 1:20-23

which he exerted in Christ when he raised him from the dead and seated him at his right hand in the heavenly realms, far above all rule and authority, power and dominion, and every title that can be given, not only in the present age but also in the one to come. And God placed all things under his feet and appointed him to be head over everything for the church, which is his body, the fullness of him who fills everything in every way.

Col. 1:18

And he is the head of the body, the church; he is the beginning and the firstborn from among the dead, so that in everything he might have the supremacy.

2 Matt. 28:18

Then Jesus came to them and said, "All authority in heaven and on earth has been given to me."

John 5:22-23

Moreover, the Father judges no one, but has entrusted all judgment to the Son, that all may honor the Son just as they honor the Father. He who does not honor the Son does not honor the Father, who sent him.

51 Q. How does this glory of Christ our head benefit us?

A. First, through his Holy Spirit
   he pours out his gifts from heaven
      upon us his members.[1]

   Second, by his power
   he defends us and keeps us safe
      from all enemies.[2]

---

1   **Acts 2:33**

Exalted to the right hand of God, he has received from the Father the promised Holy Spirit and has poured out what you now see and hear.

Eph. 4:7-12

But to each one of us grace has been given as Christ apportioned it. This is why it says:

"When he ascended on high,
   he led captives in his train
   and gave gifts to men."

(What does "he ascended" mean except that he also descended to the lower, earthly regions? He who descended is the very one who ascended higher than all the heavens, in order to fill the whole universe.) It was he who gave some to be apostles, some to be prophets, some to be evangelists, and some to be pastors and teachers, to prepare God's people for works of service, so that the body of Christ may be built up.

2   **Psalm 110:1-2**

The LORD says to my Lord:
   "Sit at my right hand
until I make your enemies
   a footstool for your feet."

The LORD will extend your mighty
      scepter from Zion;
   you will rule in the midst of your enemies.

John 10:27-30

My sheep listen to my voice; I know them, and they follow me. I give them eternal life, and they shall never perish; no one can snatch them out of my hand. My Father, who has given them to me, is greater than all; no one can snatch them out of my Father's hand. I and the Father are one.

Rev. 19:11-16

I saw heaven standing open and there before me was a white horse, whose rider is called Faithful and True. With justice he judges and makes war. His eyes are like blazing fire, and on his head are many crowns. He has a name written on him that no one knows but he himself. He is dressed in a robe dipped in blood, and his name is the Word of God. The armies of heaven were following him, riding on white horses and dressed in fine linen, white and clean. Out of his mouth comes a sharp sword with which to strike down the nations. "He will rule them with an iron scepter." He treads the winepress of the fury of the wrath of God Almighty. On his robe and on his thigh he has his name written:

KING OF KINGS AND LORD OF LORDS.

**52 Q. How does Christ's return
"to judge the living and the dead"
comfort you?**

A. In all my distress and persecution
I turn my eyes to the heavens
and confidently await as judge the very One
who has already stood trial in my place before God
and so has removed the whole curse from me.[1]
All his enemies and mine
he will condemn to everlasting punishment:
but me and all his chosen ones
he will take along with him
into the joy and the glory of heaven.[2]

[1]   Luke 21:28

When these things begin to take place, stand up and lift up your heads, because your redemption is drawing near.

Rom. 8:22-25

We know that the whole creation has been groaning as in the pains of childbirth right up to the present time. Not only so, but we ourselves, who have the firstfruits of the Spirit, groan inwardly as we wait eagerly for our adoption as sons, the redemption of our bodies. For in this hope we were saved. But hope that is seen is no hope at all. Who hopes for what he already has? But if we hope for what we do not yet have, we wait for it patiently.

Phil. 3:20-21

But our citizenship is in heaven. And we eagerly await a Savior from there, the Lord Jesus Christ, who by the power that enables him to bring everything under his control, will transform our lowly bodies so that they will be like his glorious body.

Titus 2:13-14

while we wait for the blessed hope—the glorious appearing of our great God and Savior, Jesus Christ, who gave himself for us to redeem us from all wickedness and to purify for himself a people that are his very own, eager to do what is good.

[2]   Matt. 25:31-46

"When the Son of Man comes in his glory, and all the angels with him, he will sit on his throne in heavenly glory. All the nations will be gathered before him, and he will separate the people one from another as a shepherd separates the sheep from the goats. He will put the sheep on his right and the goats on his left.

"Then the King will say to those on his right, 'Come, you who are blessed by my Father; take your inheritance, the kingdom prepared for you since the creation of the world. For I was hungry and you gave me something to eat, I was thirsty and you gave me something to drink, I was a stranger and you invited me in, I needed clothes and you clothed me, I was sick and you looked after me. I was in prison and you came to visit me.'

"Then the righteous will answer him, 'Lord, when did we see you hungry and feed you, or thirsty and give you something to drink? When did we see you a stranger and invite you in, or needing clothes and clothe you? When did we see you sick or in prison and go to visit you?'

"The King will reply, 'I tell you the truth, whatever you did for one of the least of these brothers of mine, you did for me.'

"Then he will say to those on his left, 'Depart from me, you who are cursed, into the eternal fire prepared for the devil and his angels. For I was hungry and you gave me nothing to eat, I was thirsty and you gave me nothing to drink, I was a stranger and you did not invite me in, I needed clothes and you did not clothe me, I was sick and in prison and you did not look after me.'

"They also will answer, 'Lord, when did we see you hungry or thirsty or a stranger or needing clothes or sick or in prison, and did not help you?'

"He will reply, 'I tell you the truth, whatever you did not do for one of the least of these, you did not do for me.'

"Then they will go away to eternal punishment, but the righteous to eternal life."

2 Thess. 1:6-10

God is just: He will pay back trouble to those who trouble you and give relief to you who are troubled, and to us as well. This will happen when the Lord Jesus is revealed from heaven in blazing fire with his powerful angels. He will punish those who do not know God and do not obey the gospel of our Lord Jesus. They will be punished with everlasting destruction and shut out from the presence of the Lord and from the majesty of his power on the day he comes to be glorified in his holy people and to be marveled at among all those who have believed. This includes you, because you believed our testimony to you.

LORD'S DAY 20

**53 Q. What do you believe
concerning "the Holy Spirit"?**

A. First, he, as well as the Father and the Son,
is eternal God.[1]

Second, he has been given to me personally,[2]
so that, by true faith,
he makes me share in Christ and all his blessings,[3]
comforts me,[4]
and remains with me forever.[5]

---

1   **Gen. 1:1-2**

In the beginning God created the heavens and
the earth. Now the earth was formless and
empty, darkness was over the surface of the
deep, and the Spirit of God was hovering over
the waters.

Matt. 28:19

Therefore go and make disciples of all nations,
baptizing them in the name of the Father and of
the Son and of the Holy Spirit . . . .

Acts 5:3-4

Then Peter said, "Ananias, how is it that Satan
has so filled your heart that you have lied to the
Holy Spirit and have kept for yourself some of
the money you received for the land? Didn't it
belong to you before it was sold? And after it
was sold, wasn't the money at your disposal?
What made you think of doing such a thing?
You have not lied to men but to God."

2   **1 Cor. 6:19**

Do you not know that your body is a temple
of the Holy Spirit, who is in you, whom you
have received from God? You are not your
own . . . .

2 Cor. 1:21-22

Now it is God who makes both us and you
stand firm in Christ. He anointed us, set his seal
of ownership on us, and put his Spirit in our
hearts as a deposit, guaranteeing what is to come.

Gal. 4:6

Because you are sons, God sent the Spirit of
his Son into our hearts, the Spirit who calls out,
"*Abba*, Father."

3   **Gal. 3:14**

He redeemed us in order that the blessing
given to Abraham might come to the Gentiles
through Christ Jesus, so that by faith we might
receive the promise of the Spirit.

4   **John 15:26**

When the Counselor comes, whom I will send
to you from the Father, the Spirit of truth who
goes out from the Father, he will testify about me.

Acts 9:31

Then the church throughout Judea, Galilee
and Samaria enjoyed a time of peace. It was
strengthened; and encouraged by the Holy
Spirit, it grew in numbers, living in the fear of
the Lord.

5   **John 14:16-17**

And I will ask the Father, and he will give you
another Counselor to be with you forever—the
Spirit of truth. The world cannot accept him, because it neither sees him nor knows him. But
you know him, for he lives with you and will be
in you.

1 Pet. 4:14

If you are insulted because of the name of
Christ, you are blessed, for the Spirit of glory
and of God rests on you.

54 Q. **What do you believe**
concerning "the holy catholic church"?

A. I believe that the Son of God
through his Spirit and Word,[1]
out of the entire human race,[2]
from the beginning of the world to its end,[3]
gathers, protects, and preserves for himself
a community chosen for eternal life[4]
and united in true faith.[5]
And of this community I am[6] and always will be[7]
a living member.

---

1   John 10:14-16

I am the good shepherd; I know my sheep and my sheep know me—just as the Father knows me and I know the Father—and I lay down my life for the sheep. I have other sheep that are not of this sheep pen. I must bring them also. They too will listen to my voice, and there shall be one flock and one shepherd.

Acts 20:28

Keep watch over yourselves and all the flock of which the Holy Spirit has made you overseers. Be shepherds of the church of God, which he bought with his own blood.

Rom. 10:14-17

How, then, can they call on the one they have not believed in? And how can they believe in the one of whom they have not heard? And how can they hear without someone preaching to them? And how can they preach unless they are sent? As it is written, "How beautiful are the feet of those who bring good news!"

But not all the Israelites accepted the good news. For Isaiah says, "Lord, who has believed our message?" Consequently, faith comes from hearing the message, and the message is heard through the word of Christ.

Col. 1:18

And he is the head of the body, the church; he is the beginning and the firstborn from among the dead, so that in everything he might have the supremacy.

2   Gen. 26:3b

For to you and your descendants I will give all these lands and will confirm the oath I swore to your father Abraham.

Rev. 5:9

And they sang a new song:
"You are worthy to take the scroll
and to open its seals,
because you were slain,
and with your blood you
purchased men for God
from every tribe and language and
people and nation.

3   Isa. 59:21

"As for me, this is my covenant with them," says the LORD. "My Spirit who is on you, and my words that I have put in your mouth will not depart from your mouth, or from the mouths of your children, or from the mouths of their descendants from this time on and forever," says the LORD.

1 Cor. 11:26

For whenever you eat this bread and drink the cup, you proclaim the Lord's death until he comes.

4   Matt. 16:18

And I tell you that you are Peter, and on this rock I will build my church, and the gates of Hades will not overcome it.

John 10:28-30

I give them eternal life, and they shall never perish; no one can snatch them out of my hand. My Father, who has given them to me, is greater than all; no one can snatch them out of my Father's hand. I and the Father are one.

Rom. 8:28-30

And we know that in all things God works for the good of those who love him, who have been called according to his purpose. For those God foreknew he also predestined to be conformed to the likeness of his Son, that he might be the firstborn among many brothers. And those he predestined, he also called; those he called, he also justified; those he justified, he also glorified.

Eph. 1:3-14

Praise be to the God and Father of our Lord Jesus Christ, who has blessed us in the heavenly realms with every spiritual blessing in Christ. For he chose us in him before the creation of the world to be holy and blameless in his sight. In love he predestined us to be adopted as his sons through Jesus Christ, in accordance with his pleasure and will—to the praise of his glorious grace, which he has freely given us in the One he loves. In him we have redemption through his blood, the forgiveness of sins, in accordance with the riches of God's grace that he lavished on us with all wisdom and understanding. And he made known to us the mystery of his will according to his good pleasure, which he purposed in Christ, to be put into effect when the times will have reached their fulfillment—to bring all things in heaven and on earth together under one head, even Christ.

In him we were also chosen, having been predestined according to the plan of him who works out everything in conformity with the purpose of his will, in order that we, who were the first to hope in Christ, might be for the praise of his glory. And you also were included in Christ when you heard the word of truth, the gospel of your salvation. Having believed, you were marked in him with a seal, the promised Holy Spirit, who is a deposit guaranteeing our inheritance until the redemption of those who are God's possession—to the praise of his glory.

5   Acts 2:42-47

They devoted themselves to the apostles' teaching and to the fellowship, to the breaking of bread and to prayer. Everyone was filled with awe, and many wonders and miraculous signs were done by the apostles. All the believers were together and had everything in common. Selling their possessions and goods, they gave to anyone as he had need. Every day they continued to meet together in the temple courts. They broke bread in their homes and ate together with glad and sincere hearts, praising God and enjoying the favor of all the people. And the Lord added to their number daily those who were being saved.

Eph. 4:1-6

As a prisoner for the Lord, then, I urge you to live a life worthy of the calling you have received. Be completely humble and gentle; be patient, bearing with one another in love. Make every effort to keep the unity of the Spirit through the bond of peace. There is one body and one Spirit—just as you were called to one hope when you were called—one Lord, one faith, one baptism; one God and Father of all, who is over all and through all and in all.

6   1 John 3:14

We know that we have passed from death to life, because we love our brothers. Anyone who does not love remains in death.

1 John 3:19-21

This then is how we know that we belong to the truth, and how we set our hearts at rest in his presence whenever our hearts condemn us. For God is greater than our hearts, and he knows everything.

Dear friends, if our hearts do not condemn us, we have confidence before God.

7   John 10:27-28

My sheep listen to my voice; I know them, and they follow me. I give them eternal life, and they shall never perish; no one can snatch them out of my hand.

1 Cor. 1:4-9

I always thank God for you because of his grace given you in Christ Jesus. For in him you have been enriched in every way—in all your speaking and in all your knowledge—because our testimony about Christ was confirmed in you. Therefore you do not lack any spiritual gift as you eagerly wait for our Lord Jesus Christ to be revealed. He will keep you strong to the end, so that you will be blameless on the day of our Lord Jesus Christ. God, who has called you into fellowship with his Son Jesus Christ our Lord, is faithful.

1 Pet. 1:3-5

Praise be to the God and Father of our Lord Jesus Christ! In his great mercy he has given us new birth into a living hope through the resurrection of Jesus Christ from the dead, and into an inheritance that can never perish, spoil or fade—kept in heaven for you, who through faith are shielded by God's power until the coming of the salvation that is ready to be revealed in the last time.

55 Q. What do you understand by "the communion of saints"?

A. First, that believers one and all,
as members of this community,
share in Christ
and in all his treasures and gifts.[1]

Second, that each member
should consider it a duty
to use these gifts
readily and cheerfully
for the service and enrichment
of the other members.[2]

[1] **Rom. 8:32**

He who did not spare his own Son, but gave him up for us all—how will he not also, along with him, graciously give us all things?

1 Cor. 6:17

But he who unites himself with the Lord is one with him in spirit.

1 Cor. 12:4-7

There are different kinds of gifts, but the same Spirit. There are different kinds of service, but the same Lord. There are different kinds of working, but the same God works all of them in all men.

Now to each one the manifestation of the Spirit is given for the common good.

1 Cor. 12:12-13

The body is a unit, though it is made up of many parts; and though all its parts are many, they form one body. So it is with Christ. For we were all baptized by one Spirit into one body—whether Jews or Greeks, slave or free—and we were all given the one Spirit to drink.

1 John 1:3

We proclaim to you what we have seen and heard, so that you also may have fellowship with us. And our fellowship is with the Father and with his Son, Jesus Christ.

[2] **Rom. 12:4-8**

Just as each of us has one body with many members, and these members do not all have the same function, so in Christ we who are many form one body, and each member belongs to all the others. We have different gifts, according to the grace given us. If a man's gift is prophesying, let him use it in proportion to his faith. If it is serving, let him serve; if it is teaching, let him teach; if it is encouraging, let him encourage; if it is contributing to the needs of others, let him give generously; if it is leadership, let him govern diligently; if it is showing mercy, let him do it cheerfully.

1 Cor. 12:20-27

As it is, there are many parts, but one body. The eye cannot say to the hand, "I don't need you!" And the head cannot say to the feet, "I don't need you!" On the contrary, those parts of the body that seem to be weaker are indispensable, and the parts that we think are less honorable we treat with special honor. And the parts that are unpresentable are treated with special modesty, while our presentable parts need no special treatment. But God has combined the members of the body and has given greater honor to the parts that lacked it, so that there should be no division in the body, but that its parts should have equal concern for each other. If one part suffers, every part suffers with it; if one part is honored, every part rejoices with it.

Now you are the body of Christ, and each one of you is a part of it.

1 Cor. 13:1-7

If I speak in the tongues of men and of angels, but have not love, I am only a resounding gong or a clanging cymbal. If I have the gift of prophecy and can fathom all mysteries and all knowledge, and if I have a faith that can move mountains, but have not love, I am nothing. If I give all I possess to the poor and surrender my body to the flames, but have not love, I gain nothing.

Love is patient, love is kind. It does not envy, it does not boast, it is not proud. It is not rude, it is not self-seeking, it is not easily angered, it keeps no record of wrongs. Love does not delight in evil, but rejoices with the truth. It always protects, always trusts, always hopes, always perseveres.

Phil. 2:4-8

Each of you should look not only to your own interests, but also the interests of others.

Your attitude should be the same as that of Christ Jesus:

Who, being in very nature God,
did not consider equality with God
something to be grasped,
but made himself nothing,
taking the very nature of a servant,
being made in human likeness.
And being found in appearance as a man,
he humbled himself
and became obedient to death—
even death on a cross!

56 Q. What do you believe concerning "the forgiveness of sins"?

A. I believe that God,
because of Christ's atonement,
will never hold against me
any of my sins[1]
nor my sinful nature
which I need to struggle against all my life.[2]

Rather, in his grace
God grants me the righteousness of Christ
to free me forever from judgment.[3]

[1] **Psalm 103:3, 4, 10, 12**

who forgives all your sins
and heals all your diseases,
who redeems your life from the pit
and crowns you with love and compassion
he does not treat us as our sins deserve
or repay us according to our iniquities.
as far as the east is from the west,
so far has he removed our
transgressions from us.

Mic. 7:18-19

Who is a God like you,
who pardons sin and forgives the
transgression
of the remnant of his inheritance?
You do not stay angry forever
but delight to show mercy.
You will again have compassion on us;
you will tread our sins underfoot
and hurl all our iniquities into the
depths of the sea.

2 Cor. 5:18-21

All this is from God, who reconciled us to himself through Christ and gave us the ministry of reconciliation: that God was reconciling the world to himself in Christ, not counting men's sins against them. And he has committed to us the message of reconciliation. We are therefore Christ's ambassadors, as though God were making his appeal through us. We implore you on Christ's behalf: Be reconciled to God. God made him who had no sin to be sin for us, so that in him we might become the righteousness of God.

1 John 1:7

But if we walk in the light, as he is in the light, we have fellowship with one another, and the blood of Jesus, his Son, purifies us from all sin.

1 John 2:2

He is the atoning sacrifice for our sins, and not only for ours but also for the sins of the whole world.

[2] **Rom. 7:21-25**

So I find this law at work: When I want to do good, evil is right there with me. For in my inner being I delight in God's law; but I see another law at work in the members of my body, waging war against the law of my mind and making me a prisoner of the law of sin at work within my members. What a wretched man I am! Who will rescue me from this body of death? Thanks be to God—through Jesus Christ our Lord!

So then, I myself in my mind am a slave to God's law, but in the sinful nature a slave to the law of sin.

[3] **John 3:17-18**

For God did not send his Son into the world to condemn the world, but to save the world through him. Whoever believes in him is not condemned, but whoever does not believe stands condemned already because he has not believed in the name of God's one and only Son.

Rom. 8:1-2

Therefore, there is now no condemnation for those who are in Christ Jesus, because through Christ Jesus the law of the Spirit of life set me free from the law of sin and death.

57 Q. How does "the resurrection of the body" comfort you?

A. Not only my soul
will be taken immediately after this life
to Christ its head,[1]
but even my very flesh, raised by the power of Christ,
will be reunited with my soul
and made like Christ's glorious* body.[2]

---

1   **Luke 23:43**

Jesus answered him, "I tell you the truth, today you will be with me in paradise."

Phil. 1:21-23

For to me, to live is Christ and to die is gain. If I am to go on living in the body, this will mean fruitful labor for me. Yet what shall I choose? I do not know! I am torn between the two: I desire to depart and be with Christ, which is better by far . . . .

2   **1 Cor. 15:20**

But Christ has indeed been raised from the dead, the firstfruits of those who have fallen asleep.

1 Cor. 15:42-46

So will it be with the resurrection of the dead. The body that is sown is perishable, it is raised imperishable; it is sown in dishonor, it is raised in glory; it is sown in weakness, it is raised in power; it is sown a natural body, it is raised a spiritual body.
If there is a natural body, there is also a spiritual body. So it is written: "The first man Adam became a living being"; the last Adam, a life-giving spirit. The spiritual did not come first, but the natural, and after that the spiritual.

1 Cor. 15:54

When the perishable has been clothed with the imperishable, and the mortal with immortality, then the saying that is written will come true: "Death has been swallowed up in victory."

Phil. 3:21

who, by the power that enables him to bring everything under his control, will transform our lowly bodies so that they will be like his glorious body.

1 John 3:2

Dear friends, now we are children of God, and what we will be has not yet been made known. But we know that when he appears, we shall be like him, for we shall see him as he is.

---

*The first edition had here the German word for "holy." This was later corrected to the German word for "glorious."

58 **Q.** **How does the article concerning "life everlasting" comfort you?**

A. Even as I already now
experience in my heart
the beginning of eternal joy,[1]
so after this life I will have
perfect blessedness such as
no eye has seen,
no ear has heard,
no human heart has ever imagined:
a blessedness in which to praise God eternally.[2]

---

[1] **Rom. 14:17**

For the kingdom of God is not a matter of eating and drinking, but of righteousness, peace and joy in the Holy Spirit.

[2] **John 17:3**

Now this is eternal life: that they may know you, the only true God, and Jesus Christ, whom you have sent.

1 Cor. 2:9

However, as it is written:

"No eye has seen,
no ear has heard,
no mind has conceived
what God has prepared for those who
love him"—

**59   Q.   What good does it do you, however,
to believe all this?**

   **A.   In Christ I am right with God
and heir to life everlasting.**[1]

1   **John 3:36**

Whoever believes in the Son has eternal life,
but whoever rejects the Son will not see life, for
God's wrath remains on him.

Rom. 1:17 (Hab. 2:4)

For in the gospel a righteousness from God is
revealed, a righteousness that is by faith from
first to last, just as it is written: "The righteous
will live by faith."

Rom. 5:1-2

Therefore, since we have been justified
through faith, we have peace with God through
our Lord Jesus Christ, through whom we have
gained access by faith into this grace in which
we now stand. And we rejoice in the hope of the
glory of God.

60 Q. How are you right with God?

A. Only by true faith in Jesus Christ.[1]

Even though my conscience accuses me
of having grievously sinned against all God's commandments
and of never having kept any of them,[2]
and even though I am still inclined toward all evil,[3]
nevertheless,
without my deserving it at all,[4]
out of sheer grace,[5]
God grants and credits to me
the perfect satisfaction, righteousness, and holiness of Christ,[6]
as if I had never sinned nor been a sinner,
as if I had been as perfectly obedient
as Christ was obedient for me.[7]

All I need to do
is to accept the gift of God with a believing heart.[8]

1   Rom. 3:21-28

But now a righteousness from God, apart from law, has been made known, to which the Law and the Prophets testify.

This righteousness from God comes through faith in Jesus Christ to all who believe. There is no difference, for all have sinned and fall short of the glory of God, and are justified freely by his grace through the redemption that came by Christ Jesus. God presented him as a sacrifice of atonement, through faith in his blood. He did this to demonstrate his justice, because in his forbearance he had left the sins committed beforehand unpunished—he did it to demonstrate his justice at the present time, so as to be just and the one who justifies those who have faith in Jesus.

Where, then, is boasting? It is excluded. On what principle? On that of observing the law? No, but on that of faith. For we maintain that a man is justified by faith apart from observing the law.

Gal. 2:16

know that a man is not justified by observing the law, but by faith in Jesus Christ. So we, too, have put our faith in Christ Jesus that we may be justified by faith in Christ and not by observing the law, because by observing the law no one will be justified.

Eph. 2:8-9

For it is by grace you have been saved, through faith—and this not from yourselves, it is the gift of God—not by works, so that no one can boast.

Phil. 3:8-11

What is more, I consider everything a loss compared to the surpassing greatness of knowing Christ Jesus my Lord, for whose sake I have lost all things. I consider them rubbish, that I may gain Christ and be found in him, not having a righteousness of my own that comes from the law, but that which is through faith in Christ—the righteousness that comes from God and is by faith. I want to know Christ and the power of his resurrection and the fellowship of sharing in his sufferings, becoming like him in his death, and so, somehow, to attain to the resurrection from the dead.

2   Rom. 3:9-10

What shall we conclude then? Are we any better? Not at all! We have already made the charge that Jews and Gentiles alike are all under sin. As it is written:
"There is no one righteous, not even one . . . ."

3   Rom. 7:23

but I see another law at work in the members of my body, waging war against the law of my mind and making me a prisoner of the law of sin at work within my members.

4   Tit. 3:4-5

But when the kindness and love of God our Savior appeared, he saved us, not because of righteous things we had done, but because of his mercy. He saved us through the washing of rebirth and renewal by the Holy Spirit.

5   **Rom. 3:24**

and are justified freely by his grace through the redemption that came by Christ Jesus.

Eph. 2:8

For it is by grace you have been saved, through faith—and this not from yourselves, it is the gift of God—

6   **Rom. 4:3-5 (Gen. 15:6)**

What does the Scripture say? "Abraham believed God, and it was credited to him as righteousness."

Now when a man works, his wages are not credited to him as a gift, but as an obligation. However, to the man who does not work but trusts God who justifies the wicked, his faith is credited as righteousness.

2 Cor. 5:17-19

Therefore, if anyone is in Christ, he is a new creation; the old has gone, the new has come! All this is from God, who reconciled us to himself through Christ and gave us the ministry of reconciliation: that God was reconciling the world to himself in Christ, not counting men's sins against them. And he has committed to us the message of reconciliation.

1 John 2:1-2

My dear children, I write this to you so that you will not sin. But if anybody does sin, we have one who speaks to the Father in our defense—Jesus Christ, the Righteous One. He is the atoning sacrifice for our sins, and not only for ours but also for the sins of the whole world.

7   **Rom. 4:24-25**

but also for us, to whom God will credit righteousness—for us who believe in him who raised Jesus our Lord from the dead. He was delivered over to death for our sins and was raised to life for our justification.

2 Cor. 5:21

God made him who had no sin to be sin for us, so that in him we might become the righteousness of God.

8   **John 3:18**

Whoever believes in him is not condemned, but whoever does not believe stands condemned already because he has not believed in the name of God's one and only Son.

Acts 16:30-31

He then brought them out and asked, "Sirs, what must I do to be saved?"

They replied, "Believe in the Lord Jesus, and you will be saved—you and your household."

**61 Q. Why do you say that
by faith alone
you are right with God?**

A. It is not because of any value my faith has
that God is pleased with me.
Only Christ's satisfaction, righteousness, and holiness
make me right with God.[1]
And I can receive this righteousness and make it mine
in no other way than
by faith alone.[2]

1   **1 Cor. 1:30-31**

It is because of him that you are in Christ Jesus, who has become for us wisdom from God—that is, our righteousness, holiness and redemption. Therefore, as it is written: "Let him who boasts boast in the Lord."

2   **Rom. 10:10**

For it is with your heart that you believe and are justified, and it is with your mouth that you confess and are saved.

1 John 5:10-12

Anyone who believes in the Son of God has this testimony in his heart. Anyone who does not believe God has made him out to be a liar, because he has not believed the testimony God has given about his Son. And this is the testimony; God has given us eternal life, and this life is in his Son. He who has the Son has life; he who does not have the Son of God does not have life.

62　Q.　Why can't the good we do
　　　　make us right with God,
　　　　or at least help make us right with him?

　　A.　Because the righteousness
　　　　which can pass God's scrutiny
　　　　　　must be entirely perfect
　　　　　　and must in every way measure up to the divine law.[1]
　　　　Even the very best we do in this life
　　　　　　is imperfect
　　　　　　and stained with sin.[2]

[1] **Rom. 3:20**

Therefore no one will be declared righteous in his sight by observing the law; rather, through the law we become conscious of sin.

Gal. 3:10 (Deut. 27:26)

All who rely on observing the law are under a curse, for it is written: "Cursed is everyone who does not continue to do everything written in the Book of the Law."

[2] **Isa. 64:6**

All of us have become like one who is unclean,
　　and all our righteous acts are like
　　　　filthy rags;
we all shrivel up like a leaf,
　　and like the wind our sins sweep us away.

63 Q. How can you say that the good we do doesn't earn anything when God promises to reward it in this life and the next?[1]

   A. This reward is not earned; it is a gift of grace.[2]

---

[1] **Matt. 5:12**

Rejoice and be glad, because great is your reward in heaven, for in the same way they persecuted the prophets who were before you.

Heb. 11:6

And without faith it is impossible to please God, because anyone who comes to him must believe that he exists and that he rewards those who earnestly seek him.

[2] **Luke 17:10**

"So you also, when you have done everything you were told to do, should say, 'We are unworthy servants; we have only done our duty.' "

2 Tim. 4:7-8

I have fought the good fight, I have finished the race, I have kept the faith. Now there is in store for me the crown of righteousness, which the Lord, the righteous Judge, will award to me on that day—and not only to me, but also to all who have longed for his appearing.

**64 Q. But doesn't this teaching
make people indifferent and wicked?**

A. No.
It is impossible
for those grafted into Christ by true faith
not to produce fruits of gratitude.[1]

1   Luke 6:43-45
No good tree bears bad fruit, nor does a bad tree bear good fruit. Each tree is recognized by its own fruit. People do not pick figs from thornbushes, or grapes from briers. The good man brings good things out of the good stored up in his heart, and the evil man brings evil things out of the evil stored up in his heart. For out of the overflow of his heart his mouth speaks.

John 15:5
I am the vine; you are the branches. If a man remains in me and I in him, he will bear much fruit; apart from me you can do nothing.

LORD'S DAY 25

65 Q. **It is by faith alone**
that we share in Christ and all his blessings:
where then does that faith come from?

A. The Holy Spirit produces it in our hearts[1]
by the preaching of the holy gospel,[2]
and confirms it
through our use of the holy sacraments.[3]

1   **John 3:5**

Jesus answered, "I tell you the truth, no one can enter the Kingdom of God unless he is born of water and the Spirit."

1 Cor. 2:10-14

but God has revealed it to us by his Spirit.
The Spirit searches all things, even the deep things of God. For who among men knows the thoughts of a man except the man's spirit within him? In the same way no one knows the thoughts of God except the Spirit of God. We have not received the spirit of the world but the Spirit who is from God, that we may understand what God has freely given us. This is what we speak, not in words taught us by human wisdom but in words taught by the Spirit, expressing spiritual truths in spiritual words. The man without the Spirit does not accept the things that come from the Spirit of God, for they are foolishness to him, and he cannot understand them, because they are spiritually discerned.

Eph. 2:8

For it is by grace you have been saved, through faith—and this not from yourselves, it is the gift of God—

2   **Rom. 10:17**

Consequently, faith comes from hearing the message, and the message is heard through the word of Christ.

1 Pet. 1:23-25

For you have been born again, not of perishable seed, but of imperishable, through the living and enduring word of God. For,

"All men are like grass,
and all their glory is like the flowers
of the field;
the grass withers and the flowers fall,
but the word of the Lord stands forever."

And this is the word that was preached to you.

3   **Matt. 28:19-20**

Therefore go and make disciples of all nations, baptizing them in the name of the Father and of the Son and of the Holy Spirit, and teaching them to obey everything I have commanded you. And surely I am with you always, to the very end of the age."

1 Cor. 10:16

Is not the cup of thanksgiving for which we give thanks a participation in the blood of Christ? And is not the bread that we break a participation in the body of Christ?

66 Q. What are sacraments?

A. Sacraments are holy signs and seals for us to see.
They were instituted by God so that
by our use of them
he might make us understand more clearly
the promise of the gospel,
and might put his seal on that promise.[1]

And this is God's gospel promise:
to forgive our sins and give us eternal life
by grace alone
because of Christ's one sacrifice
finished on the cross.[2]

---

[1] **Gen. 17:11**
You are to undergo circumcision, and it will be the sign of the covenant between me and you.

Deut. 30:6
The LORD your God will circumcise your hearts and the hearts of your descendants, so that you may love him with all your heart and with all your soul, and live.

Rom. 4:11
And he received the sign of circumcision, a seal of the righteousness that he had by faith while he was still uncircumcised. So then, he is the father of all who believe but have not been circumcised, in order that righteousness might be credited to them.

[2] **Matt. 26:27-28**
Then he took the cup, gave thanks and offered it to them, saying, "Drink from it, all of you. This is my blood of the covenant, which is poured out for many for the forgiveness of sins.

Acts 2:38
Peter replied, "Repent and be baptized, every one of you, in the name of Jesus Christ for the forgiveness of your sins. And you will receive the gift of the Holy Spirit."

Heb. 10:10
And by that will, we have been made holy through the sacrifice of the body of Jesus Christ once for all.

67 Q. **Are both the word and the sacraments then**
intended to focus our faith
on the sacrifice of Jesus Christ on the cross
as the only ground of our salvation?

A. Right!
In the gospel the Holy Spirit teaches us
and through the holy sacraments he assures us
that our entire salvation
rests on Christ's one sacrifice for us on the cross.[1]

1   **Rom. 6:3**   **Gal. 3:27**

Or don't you know that all of us who were   for all of you who were baptized into Christ
baptized into Christ Jesus were baptized into his   have clothed yourselves with Christ.
death?

           1 Cor. 11:26

For whenever you eat this bread and drink
this cup, you proclaim the Lord's death until he
comes.

68 Q. **How many sacraments**
    did Christ institute in the New Testament?

A. Two: baptism and the Lord's Supper.[1]

1   Matt. 28:19-20
Therefore go and make disciples of all nations,
baptizing them in the name of the Father and of
the Son and of the Holy Spirit, and teaching
them to obey everything I have commanded
you. And surely I am with you always, to the
very end of the age.

            1 Cor. 11:23-26
For I received from the Lord what I also
passed on to you: The Lord Jesus, on the night
he was betrayed, took bread, and when he had
given thanks, he broke it and said, "This is my
body, which is for you; do this in remembrance
of me." In the same way, after supper he took the
cup, saying, "This cup is the new covenant in
my blood; do this, whenever you drink it, in
remembrance of me." For whenever you eat this
bread and drink this cup, you proclaim the
Lord's death until he comes.

LORD'S DAY 26

**69 Q. How does baptism
remind you and assure you
that Christ's one sacrifice on the cross
is for you personally?**

    A. In this way:
Christ instituted this outward washing[1]
and with it gave the promise that,
    as surely as water washes away the dirt from the body,
    so certainly his blood and his Spirit
wash away my soul's impurity,
      in other words, all my sins.[2]

[1]   **Acts 2:38**

Peter replied, "Repent and be baptized, every one of you, in the name of Jesus Christ for the forgiveness of your sins. And you will receive the gift of the Holy Spirit.

[2]   **Matt. 3:11**

I baptize you with water for repentance. But after me will come one who is more powerful than I, whose sandals I am not fit to carry. He will baptize you with the Holy Spirit and with fire.

       Rom. 6:3-10

Or don't you know that all of us who were baptized into Christ Jesus were baptized into his death? We were therefore buried with him through baptism into death in order that, just as Christ was raised from the dead through the glory of the Father, we too may live a new life.

If we have been united with him like this in his death, we will certainly also be united with him in his resurrection. For we know that our old self was crucified with him so that the body of sin might be done away with, that we should no longer be slaves to sin—because anyone who has died has been freed from sin.

Now if we died with Christ, we believe that we will also live with him. For we know that since Christ was raised from the dead, he cannot die again; death no longer has mastery over him. The death he died, he died to sin once for all; but the life he lives, he lives to God.

       1 Pet. 3:21

and this water symbolizes baptism that now saves you also—not the removal of dirt from the body but the pledge of a good conscience toward God. It saves you by the resurrection of Jesus Christ.

70 Q. **What does it mean**
to be washed with Christ's blood and Spirit?

A. To be washed with Christ's blood means
that God, by grace, has forgiven my sins
because of Christ's blood
poured out for me in his sacrifice on the cross.[1]

To be washed with Christ's Spirit means
that the Holy Spirit has renewed me
and set me apart to be a member of Christ
so that more and more I become dead to sin
and increasingly live a holy and blameless life.[2]

[1] **Zech. 13:1**

On that day a fountain will be opened to the house of David and the inhabitants of Jerusalem, to cleanse them from sin and impurity.

Eph. 1:7-8

In him we have redemption through his blood, the forgiveness of sins in accordance with the riches of God's grace that he lavished on us with all wisdom and understanding.

Heb. 12:24

to Jesus the mediator of a new covenant, and to the sprinkled blood that speaks a better word than the blood of Abel.

1 Pet. 1:2

who have been chosen according to the foreknowledge of God the Father, through the sanctifying work of the Spirit, for obedience to Jesus Christ and sprinkling by his blood:
Grace and peace be yours in abundance.

Rev. 1:5

and from Jesus Christ, who is the faithful witness, the firstborn from the dead, and the ruler of the kings of the earth.

[2] **Ezek. 36:25-27**

I will sprinkle clean water on you, and you will be clean; I will cleanse you from all your impurities and from all your idols. I will give you a new heart and put a new spirit in you; I will remove from you your heart of stone and give you a heart of flesh. And I will put my Spirit in you and move you to follow my decrees and be careful to keep my laws.

John 3:5-8

Jesus answered, "I tell you the truth, no one can enter the kingdom of God unless he is born of water and the Spirit. Flesh gives birth to flesh, but the Spirit gives birth to spirit. You should not be surprised at my saying, 'You must be born again.' The wind blows wherever it pleases. You hear its sound, but you cannot tell where it comes from or where it is going. So it is with everyone born of the Spirit."

Rom. 6:4

We were therefore buried with him through baptism into death in order that, just as Christ was raised from the dead through the glory of the Father, we too may live a new life.

1 Cor. 6:11

And that is what some of you were. But you were washed, you were sanctified, you were justified in the name of the Lord Jesus Christ and by the Spirit of our God.

Col. 2:11-12

In him you were also circumcised, in the putting off of the sinful nature, not with a circumcision done by the hands of men but with the circumcision done by Christ, having been buried with him in baptism and raised with him through your faith in the power of God, who raised him from the dead.

71 Q. Where does Christ promise
that we are washed with his blood and Spirit
as surely as we are washed
with the water of baptism?

A. In the institution of baptism where he says:

"Therefore go and make disciples of all nations,
baptizing them in the name of the Father
and of the Son
and of the Holy Spirit."[1]

"Whoever believes and is baptized will be saved,
but whoever does not believe will be condemned."[2]*

This promise is repeated when Scripture calls baptism
the washing of rebirth[3] and
the washing away of sins.[4]

---

[1] **Matt. 28:19**
Therefore go and make disciples of all nations, baptizing them in the name of the Father and of the Son and of the Holy Spirit.

[2] **Mark 16:16**
Whoever believes and is baptized will be saved, but whoever does not believe will be condemned.

[3] **Tit. 3:5**
he saved us, not because of righteous things we had done, but because of his mercy. He saved us through the washing of rebirth and renewal by the Holy Spirit.

[4] **Acts 22:16**
And now what are you waiting for? Get up, be baptized and wash your sins away, calling on his name.

---

*Earlier and better manuscripts of Mark 16 omit the words, "whoever believes and is baptized . . . condemned."

72 Q. Does this outward washing with water itself wash away sins?

A. No, only Jesus Christ's blood and the Holy Spirit cleanse us from all sins.[1]

1   **Matt. 3:11**

I baptize you with water for repentance. But after me will come one who is more powerful than I, whose sandals I am not fit to carry. He will baptize you with the Holy Spirit and with fire.

1 Pet. 3:21

and this water symbolizes baptism that now saves you also—not the removal of dirt from the body but the pledge of a good conscience toward God. It saves you by the resurrection of Jesus Christ.

1 John 1:7

But if we walk in the light, as he is in the light, we have fellowship with one another, and the blood of Jesus, his Son, purifies us from all sin.

**73 Q. Why then does the Holy Spirit call baptism
the washing of rebirth and
the washing away of sins?**

A. God has good reasons for these words.
He wants to teach us that
the blood and Spirit of Christ wash away our sins
just as water washes away dirt from our bodies.[1]

But more important,
he wants to assure us, by this divine pledge and sign,
that the washing away of our sins spiritually
is as real as physical washing with water.[2]

---

[1] **1 Cor. 6:11**

And that is what some of you were. But you were washed, you were sanctified, you were justified in the name of the Lord Jesus Christ and by the Spirit of our God.

Rev. 1:5

and from Jesus Christ, who is the faithful witness, the firstborn from the dead, and the ruler of the kings of the earth.
To him who loves us and has freed us from our sins by his blood . . . .

Rev. 7:14

I answered, "Sir, you know."
And he said, "These are they who have come out of the great tribulation; they have washed their robes and made them white in the blood of the Lamb."

[2] **Acts 2:38**

Peter replied, "Repent and be baptized, every one of you, in the name of Jesus Christ for the forgiveness of your sins. And you will receive the gift of the Holy Spirit."

Rom. 6:3-4

Or don't you know that all of us who were baptized into Christ Jesus were baptized into his death? We were therefore buried with him through baptism into death in order that, just as Christ was raised from the dead through the glory of the Father, we too may live a new life.

Gal. 3:27

for all of you who were baptized into Christ have clothed yourselves with Christ.

74 Q. Should infants, too, be baptized?

A. Yes.

Infants as well as adults
are in God's covenant and are his people.[1]
They, no less than adults, are promised
the forgiveness of sin through Christ's blood
and the Holy Spirit who produces faith.[2]

Therefore, by baptism, the mark of the covenant,
infants should be received into the Christian church
and should be distinguished from the children
of unbelievers.[3]
This was done in the Old Testament by circumcision,[4]
which was replaced in the New Testament by baptism.[5]

---

1 **Gen. 17:7**

I will establish my covenant as an everlasting covenant between me and you and your descendants after you for the generations to come, to be your God and the God of your descendants after you.

Matt. 19:14

Jesus said, "Let the little children come to me, and do not hinder them, for the kingdom of heaven belongs to such as these."

2 **Isa. 44:1-3**

But now listen, O Jacob, my servant,
Israel, whom I have chosen.
This is what the LORD says—
he who made you who formed you
in the womb,
and who will help you:
Do not be afraid, O Jacob, my servant,
Jeshurun, whom I have chosen.
For I will pour water on the thirsty land,
and streams on the dry ground;
I will pour out my Spirit on your offspring,
and my blessing on your descendants.

Acts 2:38-39

Peter replied, "Repent and be baptized, every one of you, in the name of Jesus Christ for the forgiveness of your sins. And you will receive the gift of the Holy Spirit. The promise is for you and your children and for all who are far off— for all whom the Lord our God will call."

Acts 16:31

They replied, "Believe in the Lord Jesus, and you will be saved—you and your household."

3 **Acts 10:47**

Can anyone keep these people from being baptized with water? They have received the Holy Spirit just as we have.

1 Cor. 7:14

For the unbelieving husband has been sanctified through his wife, and the unbelieving wife has been sanctified through her believing husband. Otherwise your children would be unclean, but as it is, they are holy.

4 **Gen. 17:9-14**

Then God said to Abraham, "As for you, you must keep my covenant, you and your descendants after you for the generations to come. This is my covenant with you and your descendants after you, the covenant you are to keep: Every male among you shall be circumcised. You are to undergo circumcision, and it will be the sign of the covenant between me and you. For the generations to come every male among you who is eight days old must be circumcised, including those born in your household or bought with money from a foreigner—those who are not your offspring. Whether born in your household or bought with your money, they must be circumcised. My covenant in your flesh is to be an everlasting covenant. Any uncircumcised male, who has not been circumcised in the flesh, will be cut off from his people; he has broken my covenant."

5 **Col. 2:11-13**

In him you were also circumcised, in the putting off of the sinful nature, not with a circumcision done by the hands of men but with the circumcision done by Christ, having been buried with him in baptism and raised with him through your faith in the power of God, who raised him from the dead.

When you were dead in your sins and in the uncircumcision of your sinful nature, God made you alive with Christ. He forgave us all our sins.

LORD'S DAY 28

**75 Q. How does the Lord's Supper
remind you and assure you
that you share in
Christ's one sacrifice on the cross
and in all his gifts?**

A. In this way:
Christ has commanded me and all believers
to eat this broken bread and to drink this cup.
With this command he gave this promise:[1]

First,
    as surely as I see with my eyes
        the bread of the Lord broken for me
        and the cup given to me,
    so surely
        his body was offered and broken for me
        and his blood poured out for me
           on the cross.

Second,
    as surely as
        I receive from the hand of the one who serves,
    and taste with my mouth
        the bread and cup of the Lord,
        given me as sure signs of Christ's body and blood,
    so surely
        he nourishes and refreshes my soul for eternal life
        with his crucified body and poured-out blood.

---

1   **Matt. 26:26-28**

While they were eating, Jesus took bread, gave thanks and broke it, and gave it to his disciples, saying, "Take and eat; this is my body."

Then he took the cup, gave thanks and offered it to them, saying, "Drink from it, all of you. This is my blood of the covenant, which is poured out for many for the forgiveness of sins."

Mark 14:22-24

While they were eating, Jesus took bread, gave thanks and broke it, and gave it to his disciples, saying, "Take it; this is my body."

Then he took the cup, gave thanks and offered it to them, and they all drank from it.

"This is my blood of the covenant, which is poured out for many," he said to them.

Luke 22:19-20

And he took bread, gave thanks and broke it, and gave it to them, saying, "This is my body given for you; do this in remembrance of me."

In the same way, after the supper he took the cup, saying, "This cup is the new covenant in my blood, which is poured out for you."

1 Cor. 11:23-25

For I received from the Lord what I also passed on to you: The Lord Jesus, on the night he was betrayed, took bread, and when he had given thanks, he broke it and said, "This is my body, which is for you; do this in remembrance of me." In the same way, after supper he took the cup, saying, "This cup is the new covenant in my blood; do this, whenever you drink it, in remembrance of me."

**76 Q. What does it mean
to eat the crucified body of Christ
and to drink his poured-out blood?**

A. It means
to accept with a believing heart
the entire suffering and death of Christ
and by believing
to receive forgiveness of sins and eternal life.[1]

But it means more.
Through the Holy Spirit, who lives both in Christ and in us,
we are united more and more to Christ's blessed body.[2]
And so, although he is in heaven[3] and we are on earth,
we are flesh of his flesh and bone of his bone.[4]
And we forever live on and are governed by one Spirit,
as members of our body are by one soul.[5]

[1] **John 6:35**
Then Jesus declared, "I am the bread of life. He who comes to me will never go hungry, and he who believes in me will never be thirsty."

John 6:40
For my Father's will is that everyone who looks to the Son and believes in him shall have eternal life, and I will raise him up at the last day.

John 6:50-54
"But here is the bread that comes down from heaven, which a man may eat and not die. I am the living bread that came down from heaven. If anyone eats of this bread, he will live forever. This bread is my flesh, which I will give for the life of the world."
Then the Jews began to argue sharply among themselves, "How can this man give us his flesh to eat?"
Jesus said to them, "I tell you the truth, unless you eat the flesh of the Son of Man and drink his blood, you have no life in you. Whoever eats my flesh and drinks my blood has eternal life, and I will raise him up at the last day."

[2] **John 6:55-56**
For my flesh is real food and my blood is real drink. Whoever eats my flesh and drinks my blood remains in me, and I in him.

1 Cor. 12:13
For we were all baptized by one Spirit into one body—whether Jews or Greeks, slave or free—and we were all given the one Spirit to drink.

[3] **Acts 1:9-11**
After he said this, he was taken up before their very eyes, and a cloud hid him from their sight.
They were looking intently up into the sky as he was going, when suddenly two men dressed in white stood beside them. "Men of Galilee," they said, "why do you stand here looking into the sky? This same Jesus, who has been taken from you into heaven, will come back in the same way you have seen him go into heaven."

1 Cor. 11:26
For whenever you eat this bread and drink this cup, you proclaim the Lord's death until he comes.

Col. 3:1
Since then, you have been raised with Christ, set your hearts on things above, where Christ is seated at the right hand of God.

[4] **1 Cor. 6:15-17**
Do you not know that your bodies are members of Christ himself? Shall I then take the members of Christ and unite them with a prostitute? Never! Do you not know that he who unites himself with a prostitute is one with her in body? For it is said, "The two will become one flesh." But he who unites himself with the Lord is one with him in spirit.

Eph. 5:29-30
After all, no one ever hated his own body, but he feeds and cares for it, just as Christ does the church—for we are members of his body.

1 John 4:13
We know that we live in him and he in us, because he has given us of his Spirit.

5   **John 6:56-58**

Whoever eats my flesh and drinks my blood remains in me, and I in him. Just as the living Father sent me and I live because of the Father, so the one who feeds on me will live because of me. This is the bread that came down from heaven. Your forefathers ate manna and died, but he who feeds on this bread will live forever.

John 15:1-6

I am the true vine, and my Father is the gardener. He cuts off every branch in me that bears no fruit, while every branch that does bear fruit he prunes so that it will be even more fruitful. You are already clean because of the word I have spoken to you. Remain in me, and I will remain in you. No branch can bear fruit by itself; it must remain in the vine. Neither can you bear fruit unless you remain in me.

I am the vine; you are the branches. If a man remains in me and I in him, he will bear much fruit; apart from me you can do nothing. If anyone does not remain in me, he is like a branch that is thrown away and withers; such branches are picked up, thrown into the fire and burned.

Eph. 4:15-16

Instead, speaking the truth in love, we will in all things grow up into him who is the Head, that is, Christ. From him the whole body, joined and held together by every supporting ligament, grows and builds itself up in love, as each part does its work.

1 John 3:24

Those who obey his commands live in him, and he in them. And this is how we know that he lives in us: We know it by the Spirit he gave us.

77 Q. Where does Christ promise
to nourish and refresh believers
with his body and blood
as surely as
they eat this broken bread
and drink this cup?

A. In the institution of the Lord's Supper:

"The Lord Jesus, on the night he was betrayed,
took bread, and when he had given thanks,
he broke it and said,
'This is my body, which is for you;
do this in remembrance of me.'
In the same way, after supper he took the cup, saying,
'This cup is the new covenant in my blood;
do this, whenever you drink it,
in remembrance of me.'
For whenever you eat this bread and drink this cup,
you proclaim the Lord's death
until he comes."[1]

This promise is repeated by Paul in these words:

"Is not the cup of thanksgiving for which we give thanks
a participation in the blood of Christ?
And is not the bread that we break
a participation in the body of Christ?
Because there is one loaf, we, who are many, are one body,
for we all partake of the one loaf."[2]

---

[1] 1 Cor. 11:23-26

For I received from the Lord what I also passed on to you: The Lord Jesus, on the night he was betrayed, took bread, and when he had given thanks, he broke it and said, "This is my body, which is for you; do this in remembrance of me." In the same way, after supper he took the cup, saying, "This cup is the new covenant in my blood; do this, whenever you drink it, in remembrance of me." For whenever you eat this bread and drink this cup, you proclaim the Lord's death until he comes.

[2] 1 Cor. 10:16-17

Is not the cup of thanksgiving for which we give thanks a participation in the blood of Christ? And is not the bread that we break a participation in the body of Christ? Because there is one loaf, we, who are many, are one body, for we all partake of the one loaf.

78 Q. Are the bread and wine changed into the real body and blood of Christ?

    A. No.

        Just as the water of baptism
            is not changed into Christ's blood
            and does not itself wash away sins
            but is simply God's sign and assurance,[1]
        so too the bread of the Lord's Supper
            is not changed into the actual body of Christ[2]
            even though it is called the body of Christ[3]
                in keeping with the nature and language of sacraments.[4]

---

1   **Eph. 5:26**

to make her holy, cleansing her by the washing with water through the word . . . .

Tit. 3:5

he saved us, not because of righteous things we had done, but because of his mercy. He saved us through the washing of rebirth and renewal by the Holy Spirit . . . .

2   **Matt. 26:26-29**

While they were eating, Jesus took bread, gave thanks and broke it, and gave it to his disciples, saying, "Take and eat; this is my body."

Then he took the cup, gave thanks and offered it to them, saying, "Drink from it, all of you. This is my blood of the covenant, which is poured out for many for the forgiveness of sins. I tell you, I will not drink of this fruit of the vine from now on until that day when I drink it anew with you in my Father's kingdom."

3   **1 Cor. 10:16-17**

Is not the cup of thanksgiving for which we give thanks a participation in the blood of Christ? And is not the bread that we break a participation in the body of Christ? Because there is one loaf, we, who are many, are one body, for we all partake of the one loaf.

1 Cor. 11:26-28

For whenever you eat this bread and drink this cup, you proclaim the Lord's death until he comes.

Therefore, whoever eats the bread or drinks the cup of the Lord in an unworthy manner will be guilty of sinning against the body and blood of the Lord. A man ought to examine himself before he eats of the bread and drinks of the cup.

4   **Gen. 17:10-11**

This is my covenant with you and your descendants after you, the covenant you are to keep: Every male among you shall be circumcised. You are to undergo circumcision, and it will be the sign of the covenant between me and you.

Ex. 12:11, 13

This is how you are to eat it: with your cloak tucked into your belt, your sandals on your feet and your staff in your hand. Eat it in haste; it is the Lord's Passover.

The blood will be a sign for you on the houses where you are; and when I see the blood, I will pass over you. No destructive plague will touch you when I strike Egypt.

1 Cor. 10:1-4

For I do not want you to be ignorant of the fact, brothers, that our forefathers were all under the cloud and that they all passed through the sea. They were all baptized into Moses in the cloud and in the sea. They all ate the same spiritual food and drank the same spiritual drink; for they drank from the spiritual rock that accompanied them, and that rock was Christ.

79 Q. **Why then does Christ call**
the bread his body
and the cup his blood,
or the new covenant in his blood?
(Paul uses the words,
a participation in Christ's body and blood.)

A. Christ has good reason for these words.
He wants to teach us that
as bread and wine nourish our temporal life,
so too his crucified body and poured-out blood
truly nourish our souls for eternal life.[1]

But more important,
he wants to assure us, by this visible sign and pledge,
that we, through the Holy Spirit's work,
share in his true body and blood
as surely as our mouths
receive these holy signs in his remembrance,[2]
and that all of his suffering and obedience
are as definitely ours
as if we personally
had suffered and paid for our sins.[3]

---

[1]   John 6:51, 55

I am the living bread that came down from heaven. If anyone eats of this bread, he will live forever. This bread is my flesh, which I will give for the life of the world.

For my flesh is real food and my blood is real drink.

[2]   1 Cor. 10:16-17

Is not the cup of thanksgiving for which we give thanks a participation in the blood of Christ? And is not the bread that we break a participation in the body of Christ? Because there is one loaf, we, who are many, are one body, for we all partake of the one loaf.

1 Cor. 11:26

For whenever you eat this bread and drink this cup, you proclaim the Lord's death until he comes.

[3]   Rom. 6:5-11

If we have been united with him like this in his death, we will certainly also be united with him in his resurrection. For we know that our old self was crucified with him so that the body of sin might be done away with, that we should no longer be slaves to sin—because anyone who has died has been freed from sin.

Now if we died with Christ, we believe that we will also live with him. For we know that since Christ was raised from the dead, he cannot die again; death no longer has mastery over him. The death he died, he died to sin once for all; but the life he lives, he lives to God.

In the same way, count yourselves dead to sin but alive to God in Christ Jesus.

*80 Q. How does the Lord's Supper
       differ from the Roman Catholic Mass?

   A. The Lord's Supper declares to us
         that our sins have been completely forgiven
         through the one sacrifice of Jesus Christ
         which he himself finished on the cross once for all.[1]
      It also declares to us
         that the Holy Spirit grafts us into Christ,[2]
         who with his very body
         is now in heaven at the right hand of the Father[3]
         where he wants us to worship him.[4]

      But the Mass teaches
         that the living and the dead
         do not have their sins forgiven
         through the suffering of Christ
         unless Christ is still offered for them daily by the priests.
      It also teaches
         that Christ is bodily present
         in the form of bread and wine
         where Christ is therefore to be worshiped.
      Thus the Mass is basically
         nothing but a denial
         of the one sacrifice and suffering of Jesus Christ
         and a condemnable idolatry.

1   John 19:30

When he had received the drink, Jesus said,
"It is finished." With that, he bowed his head
and gave up his spirit.

Heb. 7:27

Unlike the other high priests, he does not
need to offer sacrifices day after day, first for his
own sins, and then for the sins of the people. He
sacrificed for their sins once for all when he offered himself.

Heb. 9:12, 25-26

He did not enter by means of the blood of
goats and calves; but he entered the Most Holy
Place once for all by his own blood, having obtained eternal redemption.

Nor did he enter heaven to offer himself
again and again, the way the high priest enters
the Most Holy Place every year with blood that
is not his own. Then Christ would have had to
suffer many times since the creation of the
world. But now he has appeared once for all at
the end of the ages to do away with sin by the
sacrifice of himself.

*Question and answer 80 were altogether absent from the first edition of the catechism but were
present in a shorter form in the second edition. The translation here given is of the expanded text of
the third edition.

Heb. 10:10-18

And by that will, we have been made holy through the sacrifice of the body of Jesus Christ once for all.

Day after day every priest stands and performs his religious duties; again and again he offers the same sacrifices, which can never take away sins. But when this priest had offered for all time one sacrifice for sins, he sat down at the right hand of God. Since that time he waits for his enemies to be made his footstool, because by one sacrifice he has made perfect forever those who are being made holy. The Holy Spirit also testifies to us about this. First he says:

"This is the covenant I will make with them
    after that time, says the Lord.
I will put my laws in their hearts,
    and I will write them on their minds."

Then he adds:

"Their sins and lawless acts
    I will remember no more."

And where these have been forgiven, there is no longer any sacrifice for sin.

2   **1 Cor. 6:17**

But he who unites himself with the Lord is one with him in spirit.

1 Cor. 10:16-17

Is not the cup of thanksgiving for which we give thanks a participation in the blood of Christ? And is not the bread that we break a participation in the body of Christ? Because there is one loaf, we, who are many, are one body, for we all partake of the one loaf.

3   **Acts 7:55-56**

But Stephen, full of the Holy Spirit, looked up to heaven and saw the glory of God, and Jesus standing at the right hand of God. "Look," he said, "I see heaven open and the Son of Man standing at the right hand of God."

Heb. 1:3

The Son is the radiance of God's glory and the exact representation of his being, sustaining all things by his powerful word. After he had provided purification for sins, he sat down at the right hand of the Majesty in heaven.

Heb. 8:1

The point of what we are saying is this: We do have such a high priest, who sat down at the right hand of the throne of the Majesty in heaven.

4   **Matt. 6:20-21**

But store up for yourselves treasures in heaven, where moth and rust do not destroy, and where thieves do not break in a steal. For where your treasure is, there you heart will be also.

John 4:21-24

Jesus declared, "Believe me, woman, a time is coming when you will worship the Father neither on this mountain nor in Jerusalem. You Samaritans worship what you do not know; we worship what we do know, for salvation is from the Jews. Yet a time is coming and has now come when the true worshipers will worship the Father in spirit and truth, for they are the kind of worshipers the Father seeks. God is spirit, and his worshipers must worship in spirit and in truth."

Phil. 3:20

But our citizenship is in heaven. And we eagerly await a Savior from there, the Lord Jesus Christ.

Col. 3:1-3

Since, then, you have been raised with Christ, set your hearts on things above, where Christ is seated at the right hand of God. Set your minds on things above, not on earthly things. For you died, and your life is now hidden with Christ in God.

**81 Q. Who are to come
to the Lord's table?**

A. Those who are displeased with themselves
    because of their sins,
but who nevertheless trust
    that their sins are pardoned
    and that their continuing weakness is covered
        by the suffering and death of Christ,
and who also desire more and more
    to strengthen their faith
    and to lead a better life.

Hypocrites and those who are unrepentant, however,
eat and drink judgment on themselves.[1]

1   1 Cor. 10:19-22

Do I mean then that a sacrifice offered to an idol is anything, or that an idol is anything? No, but the sacrifices of pagans are offered to demons, not to God, and I do not want you to be participants with demons. You cannot drink the cup of the Lord and the cup of demons too; you cannot have a part in both the Lord's table and the table of demons. Are we trying to arouse the Lord's jealousy? Are we stronger than he?

1 Cor. 11:26-32

For whenever you eat this bread and drink this cup, you proclaim the Lord's death until he comes.

Therefore, whoever eats the bread or drinks the cup of the Lord in an unworthy manner will be guilty of sinning against the body and blood of the Lord. A man ought to examine himself before he eats of the bread and drinks of the cup. For anyone who eats and drinks without recognizing the body of the Lord eats and drinks judgment on himself. That is why many among you are weak and sick, and a number of you have fallen asleep. But if we judged ourselves, we would not come under judgment. When we are judged by the Lord, we are being disciplined so that we will not be condemned with the world.

**82 Q. Are those to be admitted
to the Lord's Supper
who show by what they say and do
that they are unbelieving and ungodly?**

A. No, that would dishonor God's covenant
and bring down God's anger upon the entire congregation.[1]
Therefore, according to the instruction of Christ
and his apostles,
the Christian church is duty-bound to exclude such people,
by the official use of the keys of the kingdom,
until they reform their lives.

---

1   1 Cor. 11:17-32

In the following directives I have no praise for you, for your meetings do more harm than good. In the first place, I hear that when you come together as a church, there are divisions among you, and to some extent I believe it. No doubt there have to be differences among you to show which of you have God's approval. When you come together, it is not the Lord's Supper you eat, for as you eat, each of you goes ahead without waiting for anybody else. One remains hungry, another gets drunk. Don't you have homes to eat and drink in? Or do you despise the church of God and humiliate those who have nothing? What shall I say to you? Shall I praise you for this? Certainly not!

For I received from the Lord what I also passed on to you: The Lord Jesus, on the night he was betrayed, took bread, and when he had given thanks, he broke it and said, "This is my body, which is for you; do this in remembrance of me." In the same way, after supper he took the cup, saying, "This cup is the new covenant in my blood; do this, whenever you drink it, in remembrance of me." For whenever you eat this bread and drink this cup, you proclaim the Lord's death until he comes.

Therefore, whoever eats the bread or drinks the cup of the Lord in an unworthy manner will be guilty of sinning against the body and blood of the Lord. A man ought to examine himself before he eats of the bread and drinks of the cup. For anyone who eats and drinks without recognizing the body of the Lord eats and drinks judgment on himself. That is why many among you are weak and sick, and a number of you have fallen asleep. But if we judged ourselves, we would not come under judgment. When we are judged by the Lord, we are being disciplined so that we will not be condemned with the world.

Ps. 50:14-16

"Sacrifice thank offerings to God,
fulfill your vows to the Most High,
and call upon me in the day of trouble;
I will deliver you, and you will
honor me."

But to the wicked, God says:

"What right have you to recite my laws
or take my covenant on your lips?"

Isa. 1:11-17

"The multitude of your sacrifices—
what are they to me?" says the LORD.
"I have more than enough of burnt offerings,
of rams and the fat of fattened animals;
I have no pleasure
in the blood of bulls and lambs and goats.
When you come to appear before me,
who has asked this of you,
this trampling of my courts?
Stop bringing meaningless offerings!
Your incense is detestable to me.
New Moons, Sabbaths and convocations—
I cannot bear your evil assemblies.
Your New Moon festivals and your
appointed feasts
my soul hates.
They have become a burden to me;
I am weary of bearing them.
When you spread out your hands in prayer,
I will hide my eyes from you;
even if you offer many prayers,
I will not listen.
Your hands are full of blood;
wash and make yourselves clean.
Take your evil deeds
out of my sight!
Stop doing wrong,
learn to do right!
Seek justice,
encourage the oppressed.
Defend the cause of the fatherless,
plead the case of the widow.

83 **Q.** **What are the keys of the kingdom?**

A. The preaching of the holy gospel
and Christian discipline toward repentance.
Both preaching and discipline
open the kingdom of heaven to believers
and close it to unbelievers.[1]

1   Matt. 16:19   John 20:22-23
   I will give you the keys of the kingdom of   And with that he breathed on them and said,
heaven; whatever you bind on earth will be   "Receive the Holy Spirit. If you forgive anyone
bound in heaven, and whatever you loose on   his sins, they are forgiven; if you do not forgive
earth will be loosed in heaven.   them, they are not forgiven."

84 Q. How does preaching the gospel
open and close the kingdom of heaven?

A. According to the command of Christ:

The kingdom of heaven is opened
by proclaiming and publicly declaring
to all believers, each and every one, that,
as often as they accept the gospel promise in true faith,
God, because of what Christ has done,
truly forgives all their sins.

The kingdom of heaven is closed, however,
by proclaiming and publicly declaring
to unbelievers and hypocrites that,
as long as they do not repent,
the anger of God and eternal condemnation
rest on them.

God's judgment, both in this life and in the life to come,
is based on this gospel testimony.[1]

---

[1]

Matt. 16:19

I will give you the keys of the kingdom of heaven; whatever you bind on earth will be bound in heaven and whatever you loose on earth will be loosed in heaven.

John 3:31-36

The one who comes from above is above all; the one who is from the earth belongs to the earth, and speaks as one from the earth. The one whom comes from heaven is above all. He testifies to what he has seen and heard, but no one accepts his testimony. The man who has accepted it has certified that God is truthful. For the one whom God has sent speaks the words of God, for God gives the Spirit without limit. The Father loves the Son and has placed everything in his hands. Whoever believes in the Son has eternal life, but whoever rejects the Son will not see life, for God's wrath remains on him.

John 20:21-23

Again Jesus said, "Peace be with you! As the Father has sent me, I am sending you." And with that he breathed on them and said, "Receive the Holy Spirit. If you forgive anyone his sins, they are forgiven; if you do not forgive them, they are not forgiven."

85 Q. How is the kingdom of heaven closed and opened by Christian discipline?

A. According to the command of Christ:

Those who, though called Christians,
   profess unchristian teachings or live unchristian lives,
and after repeated and loving counsel
   refuse to abandon their errors and wickedness,
and after being reported to the church, that is, to its officers,
   fail to respond also to their admonition—
such persons the officers exclude
      from the Christian fellowship
   by withholding the sacraments from them,
and God himself excludes them from the kingdom of Christ.[1]

Such persons,
   when promising and demonstrating genuine reform,
are received again
      as members of Christ
      and of his church.[2]

---

[1]   Matt. 18:15-20

If your brother sins against you, go and show him his fault, just between the two of you. If he listens to you, you have won your brother over. But if he will not listen, take one or two others along, so that "every matter may be established by the testimony of two or three witnesses." If he refuses to listen to them, tell it to the church; and if he refuses to listen even to the church, treat him as you would a pagan or a tax collector.

I tell you the truth, whatever you bind on earth will be bound in heaven, and whatever you loose on earth will be loosed in heaven.

Again, I tell you that if two of you on earth agree about anything you ask for, it will be done for you by my Father in heaven. For where two or three come together in my name, there am I with them.

1 Cor. 5:3-5

Even though I am not physically present, I am with you in spirit. And I have already passed judgment on the one who did this, just as if I were present. When you are assembled in the name of our Lord Jesus and I am with you in spirit, and the power of our Lord Jesus is present, hand this man over to Satan, so that the sinful nature may be destroyed and his spirit saved on the day of the Lord.

1 Cor. 5:11-13

But now I am writing you that you must not associate with anyone who calls himself a brother but is sexually immoral or greedy, an idolater or a slanderer, a drunkard or a swindler. With such a man do not even eat.

What business is it of mine to judge those outside the church? Are you not to judge those inside? God will judge those outside. "Expel the wicked man from among you."

2 Thess. 3:14-15

If anyone does not obey our instruction in this letter, take special note of him. Do not associate with him, in order that he may feel ashamed. Yet do not regard him as an enemy, but warn him as a brother.

So he got up and went to his father.

But while he was still a long way off, his father saw him and was filled with compassion for him; he ran to his son, threw his arms around him and kissed him.

The son said to him, "Father, I have sinned against heaven and against you. I am no longer worthy to be called your son."

But the father said to his servants, "Quick! Bring the best robe and put it on him. Put a ring on his finger and sandals on his feet. Bring the fattened calf and kill it. Let's have a feast and celebrate. For this son of mine was dead and is alive again; he was lost and is found." So they began to celebrate.

The punishment inflicted on him by the majority is sufficient for him. Now instead, you ought to forgive and comfort him, so that he will not be overwhelmed by excessive sorrow. I urge you, therefore, to reaffirm your love for him. The reason I wrote you was to see if you would stand the test and be obedient in everything. If you forgive anyone, I also forgive him. And what I have forgiven—if there was anything to forgive—I have forgiven in the sight of Christ for your sake, in order that Satan might not outwit us. For we are not unaware of his schemes.

LORD'S DAY 32

86 Q. **We have been delivered**
from our misery
by God's grace alone through Christ
and not because we have earned it:
why then must we still do good?

A. To be sure, Christ has redeemed us by his blood.
But we do good because
Christ by his Spirit is also renewing us to be like himself,
so that in all our living
we may show that we are thankful to God
for all he has done for us,[1]
and so that he may be praised through us.[2]

And we do good
so that we may be assured of our faith by its fruits,[3]
and so that by our godly living
our neighbors may be won over to Christ.[4]

---

1   **Rom. 6:13**

Do not offer the parts of your body to sin, as instruments of wickedness, but rather offer yourselves to God, as those who have been brought from death to life; and offer the parts of your body to him as instruments of righteousness.

Rom. 12:1-2

Therefore, I urge you, brothers, in view of God's mercy, to offer your bodies as living sacrifices, holy and pleasing to God—this is your spiritual act of worship. Do not conform any longer to the pattern of this world, but be transformed by the renewing of your mind. Then you will be able to test and approve what God's will is—his good, pleasing and perfect will.

1 Pet. 2:5-10

you also, like living stones, are being built into a spiritual house to be a holy priesthood, offering spiritual sacrifices acceptable to God through Jesus Christ. For in Scripture it says:

"See, I lay a stone in Zion,
a chosen and precious cornerstone,
and the one who trusts in him
will never be put to shame."

Now to you who believe, this stone is precious. But to those who do not believe,

"The stone the builders rejected
has become the capstone,"

and,

"A stone that causes men to stumble
and a rock that makes them fall."

They stumble beause they disobey the message—which is also what they were destined for.

But you are a chosen people, a royal priesthood, a holy nation, a people belonging to God, that you may declare the praises of him who called you out of darkness into his wonderful light. Once you were not a people, but now you are the people of God; once you had not received mercy, but now you have received mercy.

2   **Matt. 5:16**

In the same way, let your light shine before men, that they may see your good deeds and praise your Father in heaven.

1 Cor. 6:19-20

Do you not know that your body is a temple of the Holy Spirit, who is in you, whom you have received from God? You are not your own; you were bought at a price. Therefore honor God with your body.

3   **Matt. 7:17-18**

Likewise every good tree bears good fruit, but a bad tree bears bad fruit. A good tree cannot bear bad fruit, and a bad tree cannot bear good fruit.

Gal. 5:22-24

But the fruit of the Spirit is love, joy, peace, patience, kindness, goodness, faithfulness, gentleness and self-control. Against such things there is no law. Those who belong to Christ Jesus have crucified the sinful nature with its passions and desires.

2 Pet. 1:10-11

Therefore, my brothers, be all the more eager to make your calling and election sure. For if you do these things, you will never fall, and you will receive a rich welcome into the eternal kingdom of our Lord and Savior Jesus Christ.

4   **Matt. 5:14-16**

You are the light of the world. A city on a hill cannot be hidden. Neither do people light a lamp and put it under a bowl. Instead they put it on its stand, and it gives light to everyone in the house. In the same way, let your light shine before men, that they may see your good deeds and praise your Father in heaven.

Rom. 14:17-19

For the kingdom of God is not a matter of eating and drinking, but of righteousness, peace and joy in the Holy Spirit, because anyone who serves Christ in this way is pleasing to God and approved by men.

Let us therefore make every effort to do what leads to peace and to mutual edification.

1 Pet. 2:12

Live such good lives among the pagans that, though they accuse you of doing wrong, they may see your good deeds and glorify God on the day he visits us.

1 Pet. 3:1-2

Wives, in the same way be submissive to your husbands so that, if any of them do not believe the word, they may be won over without words by the behavior of their wives, when they see the purity and reverence of your lives.

87 Q. Can those be saved
who do not turn to God
from their ungrateful
and impenitent ways?

A. By no means.
Scripture tells us that
no unchaste person,
no idolater, adulterer, thief,
no covetous person,
no drunkard, slanderer, robber,
or the like
is going to inherit the kingdom of God.[1]

1   1 Cor. 6:9-10

Do you not know that the wicked will not inherit the kingdom of God? Do not be deceived: Neither the sexually immoral nor idolaters nor adulterers nor male prostitutes nor homosexual offenders nor thieves nor the greedy nor drunkards nor slanderers nor swindlers will inherit the kingdom of God.

Gal. 5:19-21

The acts of the sinful nature are obvious: sexual immorality, impurity and debauchery; idolatry and witchcraft; hatred, discord, jealousy, fits of rage, selfish ambition, dissensions, factions and envy; drunkenness, orgies, and the like. I warn you, as I did before, that those who live like this will not inherit the kingdom of God.

Eph. 5:1-20

Be imitators of God, therefore, as dearly loved children and live a life of love, just as Christ loved us and gave himself up for us as a fragrant offering and sacrifice to God.

But among you there must not be even a hint of sexual immorality, or of any kind of impurity, or of greed, because these are improper for God's holy people. Nor should there be obscenity, foolish talk or coarse joking, which are out of place, but rather thanksgiving. For of this you can be sure: No immoral, impure or greedy person—such a man is an idolater—has any inheritance in the kingdom of Christ and of God. Let no one deceive you with empty words, for because of such things God's wrath comes on those who are disobedient. Therefore do not be partners with them.

For you were once darkness, but now you are light in the Lord. Live as children of light (for the fruit of the light consists in all goodness, righteousness and truth) and find out what pleases the Lord. Have nothing to do with fruitless deeds of darkness, but rather expose them. For it is shameful even to mention what the disobedient do in secret. But everything exposed by the light becomes visible, for it is light that makes everything visible. This is why it is said:

"Wake up, O sleeper,
rise from the dead,
and Christ will shine on you."

Be very careful, then, how you live—not as unwise but as wise, making the most of every opportunity, because the days are evil. Therefore do not be foolish, but understand what the Lord's will is. Do not get drunk on wine, which leads to debauchery. Instead, be filled with the Spirit. Speak to one another with psalms, hymns and spiritual songs. Sing and make music in your heart to the Lord, always giving thanks to God the Father for everything, in the name of our Lord Jesus Christ.

1 John 3:14

We know that we have passed from death to life, because we love our brothers. Anyone who does not love remains in death.

**88 Q. What is involved
in genuine repentance or conversion?**

A. Two things:
the dying-away of the old self,
and the coming-to-life of the new.[1]

1   Rom. 6:1-11

What shall we say, then? Shall we go on sinning so that grace may increase? By no means! We died to sin; how can we live in it any longer? Or don't you know that all of us who were baptized into Christ Jesus were baptized into his death? We were therefore buried with him through baptism into death in order that just as Christ was raised from the dead through the glory of the Father, we too may live a new life.

If we have been united with him like this in his death, we will certainly also be united with him in his resurrection. For we know that our old self was crucified with him so that the body of sin might be done away with, that we should no longer be slaves to sin— because anyone who has died has been freed from sin.

Now if we died with Christ, we believe that we will also live with him. For we know that since Christ was raised from the dead, he cannot die again; death no longer has mastery over him. The death he died, he died to sin once for all; but the life he lives, he lives to God.

In the same way, count yourselves dead to sin but alive to God in Christ Jesus.

2 Cor. 5:17

Therefore, if anyone is in Christ, he is a new creation; the old has gone, the new has come!

Eph. 4:22-24

You were taught, with regard to your former way of life, to put off your old self, which is being corrupted by its deceitful desires; to be made new in the attitude of your minds; and to put on the new self, created to be like God in true righteousness and holiness.

Col. 3:5-10

Put to death, therefore, whatever belongs to your earthly nature: sexual immorality, impurity, lust, evil desires and greed, which is idolatry. Because of these, the wrath of God is coming. You used to walk in these ways, in the life you once lived. But now you must rid yourselves of all such things as these: anger, rage, malice, slander, and filthy language from your lips. Do not lie to each other, since you have taken off your old self with its practices and have put on the new self, which is being renewed in knowledge in the image of its Creator.

89 Q. What is the dying-away of the old self?

A. It is to be genuinely sorry for sin,
to hate it more and more,
and to run away from it.[1]

1   **Ps. 51:3-4**

For I know my transgressions,
   and my sin is always before me.
Against you, you only, have I sinned
   and done what is evil in your sight,
so that you are proved right when you speak
   and justified when you judge.

Ps. 51:17

The sacrifices of God are a broken spirit;
   a broken and contrite heart,
   O God, you will not despise.

Joel 2:12-13

"Even now," declares the LORD,
   "return to me with all your heart,
   with fasting and weeping and mourning."

Rend your heart
   and not your garments.
Return to the LORD your God,
   for he is gracious and compassionate,
slow to anger and abounding in love,
   and he relents from sending calamity.

Rom. 8:12-13

Therefore, brothers, we have an obligation—but it is not to the sinful nature, to live according to it. For if you live according to the sinful nature, you will die; but if by the Spirit you put to death the misdeeds of the body, you will live,

2 Cor. 7:10

Godly sorrow brings repentance that leads to salvation and leaves no regret, but worldly sorrow brings death.

90 Q. What is the coming-to-life of the new self?

A. It is wholehearted joy in God through Christ[1]
and a delight to do every kind of good
as God wants us to.[2]

[1]   **Ps. 51:8, 12**
Let me hear joy and gladness;
let the bones you have crushed rejoice.
Restore to me the joy of your salvation
and grant me a willing spirit, to sustain me.

Isa. 57:15
For this is what the high and lofty One says—
he who lives forever, whose name is holy;
"I live in a high and holy place,
but also with him who is contrite
and lowly in spirit,
to revive the spirit of the lowly
and to revive the heart of the contrite."

Rom. 5:1
Therefore, since we have been justified
through faith, we have peace with God through
our Lord Jesus Christ,

Rom. 14:17
For the kingdom of God is not a matter of
eating and drinking, but of righteousness, peace
and joy in the Holy Spirit,

[2]   **Rom. 6:10-11**
The death he died, he died to sin once for all;
but the life he lives, he lives to God.
In the same way, count yourselves dead to sin
but alive to God in Christ Jesus.

Gal. 2:20
I have been crucified with Christ and I no
longer live, but Christ lives in me. The life I live
in the body, I live by faith in the Son of God, who
loved me and gave himself for me.

91 Q. What do we do that is good?

   A. Only that which
        arises out of true faith,[1]
        conforms to God's law,[2]
        and is done for his glory;[3]
    and not that which is based
    on what we think is right
    or on established human tradition.[4]

1   **John 15:5**

I am the vine; you are the branches. If a man remains in me and I in him, he will bear much fruit; apart from me you can do nothing.

Heb. 11:6

And without faith it is impossible to please God, because anyone who comes to him must believe that he exists and that he rewards those who earnstly seek him.

2   **Lev. 18:4**

You must obey my laws and be careful to follow my decrees. I am the Lord your God.

1 Sam. 15:22

But Samuel replied:

"Does the Lord delight in burnt
        offerings and sacrifices
    as much as in obeying the voice of the Lord?
To obey is better than sacrifice,
    and to heed is better than the fat of rams."

Eph. 2:10

For we are God's workmanship, created in Christ Jesus to do good works, which God prepared in advance for us to do.

3   **1 Cor. 10:31**

So whether you eat or drink or whatever you do, do it all for the glory of God.

4   **Deut. 12:32**

See that you do all I command you; do not add to it or take away from it.

Isa. 29:13

The Lord says:

"These people come near to me with their mouth
    and honor me with their lips,
    but their hearts are far from me.
Their worship of me
    is made up only of rules taught by men."

Ezek. 20:18-19

I said to their children in the desert, "Do not follow the statutes of your fathers or keep their laws or defile yourselves with their idols. I am the Lord your God; follow my decrees and be careful to keep my laws.

Matt. 15:7-9

You hypocrites! Isaiah was right when he prophesied about you:

"These people honor me with their lips,
    but their hearts are far from me.
They worship me in vain;
    their teachings are but rules taught by men."

92 **Q. What does the Lord say in his law?**

   A. God spoke all these words:

> *The First Commandment*
> I am the LORD your God,
>   who brought you out of Egypt,
>   out of the land of slavery.
> You shall have no other gods before me.

> *The Second Commandment*
> You shall not make for yourself an idol
>   in the form of anything in heaven above
>   or on the earth beneath
>   or in the waters below.
> You shall not bow down to them or worship them;
>   for I, the LORD your God, am a jealous God,
>   punishing the children for the sin of the fathers
>   to the third and fourth generation
>   of those who hate me,
>   but showing love to a thousand generations of those
>   who love me and keep my commandments.

> *The Third Commandment*
> You shall not misuse the name of the LORD your God,
>   for the LORD will not hold anyone guiltless
>   who misues his name.

> *The Fourth Commandment*
> Remember the Sabbath day by keeping it holy.
> Six days you shall labor and do all you work,
> but the seventh day is a Sabbath to the LORD your God.
> On it you shall not do any work,
>   neither you, nor your son or daughter,
>   nor your manservant or maidservant,
>   nor your animals,
>   nor the alien within your gates.
> For in six days the LORD made
>   the heavens and the earth, the sea,
>   and all that is in them,
> but he rested on the seventh day.
> Therefore the LORD blessed the Sabbath day
> and made it holy.

The Fifth Commandment
Honor your father and your mother,
    so that you may live long
    in the land the Lord your God is giving you.

The Sixth Commandment
You shall not murder.

The Seventh Commandment
You shall not commit adultery.

The Eighth Commandment
You shall not steal.

The Ninth Commandment
You shall not give false testimony
    against your neighbor.

The Tenth Commandment
You shall not covet your neighbor's house.
You shall not covet your neighbor's wife,
    or his manservant or maidservant,
    his ox or donkey,
    or anything that belongs to your neighbor.[1]

---

1   **Ex. 20:1-17**

And God spoke all these words:

"I am the Lord your God, who brought you out of Egypt, out of the land of slavery.

"You shall have no other gods before me.

"You shall not make for yourself an idol in the form of anything in heaven above or on the earth beneath or in the waters below. You shall not bow down to them or worship them; for I, the Lord your God, am a jealous God, punishing the children for the sin of the fathers to the third and fourth generation of those who hate me, but showing love to a thousand generations of those who love me and keep my commandments.

"You shall not misuse the name of the Lord your God, for the Lord will not hold anyone guiltless who misuses his name.

"Remember the Sabbath day by keeping it holy. Six days you shall labor and do all your work, but the seventh day is a Sabbath to the Lord your God. On it you shall not do any work, neither you, nor your son or daughter, nor your manservant or maidservant, nor your animals, nor the alien within your gates. For in six days the Lord made the heavens and the earth, the sea, and all that is in them, but he rested on the seventh day. Therefore the Lord blessed the Sabbath day and made it holy.

"Honor your father and your mother, so that you may live long in the land the Lord your God is giving you.

"You shall not murder.

"You shall not commit adultery.

"You shall not steal.

"You shall not give false testimony against your neighbor.

"You shall not covet your neighbor's house. You shall not covet your neighbor's wife, or his manservant or maidservant, his ox or donkey, or anything that belongs to your neighbor."

Deut. 5:6-21

I am the Lord your God, who
    brought you out of Egypt, out of
    the land of slavery.

You shall have no other gods before me.

You shall not make for yourself an idol in the form of anything in heaven above or on the earth beneath or in the waters below. You shall not bow down to them or worship them; for I, the Lord your God, am a jealous God, punishing the children for the sin of the fathers to the third and fourth generation of those who hate me, but showing love to a thousand generations of those who love me and keep my commandments.

You shall not misuse the name of the Lord your God, for the Lord will not hold anyone guiltless who misuses his name.

Observe the Sabbath day by keeping it holy, as the Lord your God has commanded you. Six days you shall labor and do all your work, but the seventh day is a Sabbath to the Lord your God. On it you shall not do any work, neither you, nor your son or daughter, nor your manservant or maidservant, nor your ox, your donkey or any of your animals, nor the alien within your gates, so that your manservant and maidservant may rest, as you do. Remember that you were slaves in Egypt and that the Lord your God brought you out of there with a mighty hand and an outstretched arm.

Therefore the Lord your God has commanded you to observe the Sabbath day.

Honor your father and your mother, as the Lord your God has commanded you, so that you may live long and that it may go well with you in the land the Lord your God is giving you.

You shall not murder.

You shall not commit adultery.

You shall not steal.

You shall not give false testimony against your neighbor.

You shall not covet your neighbor's wife. You shall not set your desire on your neighbor's house or land, his manservant or maidservant, his ox or donkey, or anything that belongs to your neighbor.

93 Q. How are these commandments divided?

    A. Into two tables.
        The first has four commandments,
            teaching us what our relation to God should be.
        The second has six commandments,
            teaching us what we owe our neighbor.[1]

1   Matt. 22:37-39

Jesus replied: " 'Love the Lord your God with all your heart and with all your soul and with all your mind.' This is the first and greatest commandment. And the second is like it: 'Love your neighbor as yourself.' All the Law and the Prophets hang on these two commandments."

**94 Q. What does the Lord require
in the first commandment?**

A. That I, not wanting to endanger my very salvation,
avoid and shun
all idolatry,[1] magic, superstitious rites,[2]
and prayer to saints or to other creatures.[3]

That I sincerely acknowledge the only true God,[4]
trust him alone,[5]
look to him for every good thing[6]
humbly[7] and patiently,[8]
love him,[9] fear him,[10] and honor him[11]
with all my heart.

In short,
that I give up anything
rather than go against his will in any way.[12]

[1]   **1 Cor. 6:9-10**

Do you not know that the wicked will not inherit the kingdom of God? Do not be deceived: Neither the sexually immoral nor idolaters nor adulterers nor male prostitutes nor homosexual offenders nor thieves nor the greedy nor drunkards nor slanderers nor swindlers will inherit the kingdom of God.

1 Cor. 10:5-14

Nevertheless, God was not pleased with most of them; their bodies were scattered over the desert.

Now these things occurred as examples to keep us from setting our hearts on evil things as they did. Do not be idolaters, as some of them were; as it is written: "The people sat down to eat and drink and got up to indulge in pagan revelry." We should not commit sexual immorality, as some of them did—and in one day twenty-three thousand of them died. We should not test the Lord, as some of them did—and were killed by snakes. And do not grumble, as some of them did—and were killed by the destroying angel.

These things happened to them as examples and were written down as warnings for us, on whom the fulfillment of the ages has come. So, if you think you are standing firm, be careful that you don't fall! No temptation has seized you except what is common to man. And God is faithful; he will not let you be tempted beyond what you can bear. But when you are tempted, he will also provide a way out so that you can stand up under it.

Therefore, my dear friends, flee from idolatry.

1 John 5:21

Dear children, keep yourselves from idols.

[2]   **Lev. 19:31**

Do not turn to mediums or seek out spiritists, for you will be defiled by them. I am the LORD your God.

Deut. 18:9-12

When you enter the land the LORD your God is giving you, do not learn to imitate the detestable ways of the nations there. Let no one be found among you who sacrifices his son or daughter in the fire, who practices divination or sorcery, interprets omens, engages in witchcraft, or casts spells, or who is a medium or spiritist or who consults the dead. Anyone who does these things is detestable to the LORD, and because of these detestable practices the LORD your God will drive out those nations before you.

[3]   **Matt. 4:10**

Jesus said to him, "Away from me, Satan! For it is written: 'Worship the Lord your God, and serve him only.' "

Rev. 19:10

At this I fell at his feet to worship him. But he said to me, "Do not do it! I am a fellow servant with you and with your brothers who hold the testimony of Jesus. Worship God! For the testimony of Jesus is the spirit of prophecy."

Rev. 22:8-9

I, John, am the one who heard and saw these things. And when I had heard and seen them, I fell down to worship at the feet of the angel who had been showing them to me. But he said to me, "Do not do it! I am a fellow servant with you and with your brothers the prophets and of all who keep the words of this book. Worship God!"

4 **John 17:3**

Now this is eternal life: that they may know you, the only true God, and Jesus Christ, whom you have sent.

5 **Jer. 17:5, 7**

This is what the LORD says:

"Cursed is the one who trusts in man,
    who depends on flesh for his strength
    and whose heart turns away from the LORD

"But blessed is the man who trusts in the LORD,
    whose confidence is in him."

6 **Ps. 104:27-28**

These all look to you
    to give them their food at the proper time.
When you give it to them,
    they gather it up;
when you open your hand,
    they are satisfied with good things.

James 1:17

Every good and perfect gift is from above, coming down from the Father of the heavenly lights, who does not change like shifting shadows.

7 **1 Pet. 5:5-6**

Young men, in the same way be submissive to those who are older. All of you, clothe yourselves with humility toward one another, because,

"God opposes the proud
    but gives grace to the humble."

Humble yourselves, therefore, under God's mighty hand, that he may lift you up in due time.

8 **Col. 1:11**

being strengthened with all power according to his glorious might so that you may have great endurance and patience . . . .

Heb. 10:36

You need to persevere so that when you have done the will of God, you will receive what he has promised.

9 **Matt. 22:37 (Deut. 6:5)**

Jesus replied: " 'Love the Lord your God with all your heart and with all your soul and with all your mind.' "

10 **Prov. 9:10**

The fear of the LORD is the beginning of wisdom,
    and knowledge of the Holy One is
        understanding.

1 Pet. 1:17

Since you call on a Father who judges each man's work impartially, live your lives as strangers here in reverent fear.

11 **Matt. 4:10 (Deut. 6:13)**

Jesus said to him, "Away from me, Satan! For it is written: 'Worship the Lord your God, and serve him only.' "

12 **Matt. 5:29-30**

If your right eye causes you to sin, gouge it out and throw it away. It is better for you to lose one part of your body than for your whole body to be thrown into hell. And if your right hand causes you to sin, cut it off and throw it away. It is better for you to lose one part of your body than for your whole body to go into hell.

Matt. 10:37-39

Anyone who loves his father or mother more than me is not worthy of me; anyone who loves his son or daughter more than me is not worthy of me; and anyone who does not take his cross and follow me is not worthy of me. Whoever finds his life will lose it, and whoever loses his life for my sake will find it.

95 Q. What is idolatry?

A. Idolatry is
    having or inventing something in which one trusts
    in place of or alongside of the only true God,
    who has revealed himself in his Word.[1]

1   **1 Chron. 16:26**

For all the gods of the nations are idols,
 but the Lord made the heavens.

Gal. 4:8-9

Formerly, when you did not know God, you were slaves to those who by nature are not gods. But now that you know God—how is it that you are turning back to those weak and miserable principles? Do you wish to be enslaved by them all over again?

Eph. 5:5

For of this you can be sure: No immoral, impure or greedy person—such a man is an idolater—has any inheritance in the kingdom of Christ and of God.

Phil. 3:19

Their destiny is destruction, their god is their stomach, and their glory is in their shame. Their mind is on earthly things.

**96 Q. What is God's will for us
in the second commandment?**

A. That we in no way make any image of God[1]
nor worship him in any other way
than he has commanded in his Word.[2]

1   **Deut. 4:15-19**

You saw no form of any kind the day the LORD spoke to you at Horeb out of the fire. Therefore watch yourselves very carefully, so that you do not become corrupt and make for yourselves an idol, an image of any shape, whether formed like a man or a woman, or like any animal on earth or any bird that flies in the air, or like any creature that moves along the ground or any fish in the waters below. And when you look up to the sky and see the sun, the moon and the stars—all the heavenly array—do not be enticed into bowing down to them and worshiping things the LORD your God has apportioned to all the nations under heaven.

Isa. 40:18-25

To whom, then, will you compare God?
    What image will you compare him to?
As for an idol, a craftsman casts it,
    and a goldsmith overlays it with gold
    and fashions silver chains for it.
A man too poor to present such an offering
    selects wood that will not rot.
He looks for a skilled craftsman
    to set up an idol that will not topple.
Do you not know?
    Have you not heard?
Has it not been told you from the beginning?
    Have you not understood since the
        earth was founded?
He sits enthroned above the circle of the earth,
    and its people are like grasshoppers.
He stretches out the heavens like a canopy,
    and spreads them out like a tent to live in.
He brings princes to naught
    and reduces the rulers of this world
        to nothing.
No sooner are they planted,
    no sooner are they sown,
    no sooner do they take root in the ground,
than he blows on them and they wither,
    and a whirlwind sweeps them away
        like chaff.
"To whom will you compare me?
    Or who is my equal?" says the Holy One.

Acts 17:29

Therefore since we are God's offspring, we should not think that the divine being is like gold or silver or stone—an image made by man's design and skill.

Rom. 1:22-23

Although they claimed to be wise, they became fools and exchanged the glory of the immortal God for images made to look like mortal man and birds and animals and reptiles.

2   **Lev. 10:1-7**

Aaron's son Nadab and Abihu took their censers, put fire in them and added incense; and they offered unauthorized fire before the LORD, contrary to his command. So fire came out from the presence of the LORD and consumed them, and they died before the LORD. Moses then said to Aaron, "This is what the LORD spoke of when he said:

" 'Among those who approach me
    I will show myself holy;
    in the sight of all the people
    I will be honored.' "

Aaron remained silent.

Moses summoned Mishael and Elzphan, sons of Aaron's uncle Uzziel, and said to them, "Come here; carry your cousins outside the camp, away from the front of the sanctuary." So they came and carried them, still in their tunics, outside the camp, as Moses ordered.

Then Moses said to Aaron and his sons Eleazar and Ithamar, "Do not let your hair become unkempt, and do not tear your clothes, or you will die and the LORD will be angry with the whole community. But your relatives, all the house of Israel, may mourn for those the LORD has destroyed by fire. Do not leave the entrance to the Tent of Meeting or you will die, because the LORD's anointing oil is on you." So they did as Moses said.

1 Sam. 15:22-23

But Samuel replied:

"Does the Lord delight in burnt offerings
    and sacrifices
  as much as in obeying the voice of the LORD?
To obey is better than sacrifice,
  and to heed is better than the fat of rams.
For rebellion is like the sin of divination,
  and arrogance like the evil of idolatry.
Because you have rejected the word of
      the LORD,
  he has rejected you as king."

John 4:23-24

Yet a time is coming and has now come when the true worshipers will worship the Father in spirit and truth, for they are the kind of worshipers the Father seeks. God is spirit, and his worshipers must worship in spirit and in truth.

**97 Q. May we then not make
any image at all?**

**A. God can not and may not
be visibly portrayed in any way.**

Although creatures may be portrayed,
yet God forbids making or having such images
if one's intention is to worship them
or to serve God through them.[1]

---

1 **Ex. 34:13-14, 17**
Break down their altars, smash their sacred stones and cut down their Asherah poles. Do not worship any other god, for the LORD, whose name is Jealous, is a jealous God.

Do not make cast idols.

2 Kings 18:4-5
He removed the high places, smashed the sacred stones and cut down the Asherah poles. He broke into pieces the bronze snake Moses had made, for up to that time the Israelites had been burning incense to it. (It was called Nehushtan.)

Hezekiah trusted in the LORD, the God of Israel. There was no one like him among all the kings of Judah, either before him or after him.

98 Q. But may not images be permitted in the churches as teaching aids for the unlearned?

A. No, we shouldn't try to be wiser than God.
He wants his people instructed
by the living preaching of his Word—[1]
not by idols that cannot even talk.[2]

1   **Rom. 10:14-15, 17**

How, then, can they call on the one they have not believed in? And how can they believe in the one of whom they have not heard? And how can they hear without someone preaching to them? And how can they preach unless they are sent? As it is written, "How beautiful are the feet of those who bring good news!"

Consequently, faith comes from hearing the message, and the message is heard through the word of Christ.

2 Tim. 3:16-17

All Scripture is God-breathed and is useful for teaching, rebuking, correcting and training in righteousness, so that the man of God may be thoroughly equipped for every good work.

2 Pet. 1:19

And we have the word of the prophets made more certain, and you will do well to pay attention to it, as to a light shining in a dark place, until the day dawns and the morning star rises in your hearts.

2   **Jer. 10:8**

They are all senseless and foolish;
they are taught by worthless wooden idols.

Hab. 2:18-20

Of what value is an idol, since a
man has carved it?
Or an image that teaches lies?
For he who makes it trusts in his own creation;
he makes idols that cannot speak.
Woe to him who says to wood, "Come
to life!"
Or to lifeless stone, "Wake up!"
Can it give guidance?
It is covered with gold and silver;
there is not breath in it.
But the LORD is in his holy temple;
let all the earth be silent before him.

**99 Q. What is God's will for us
in the third commandment?**

A. That we neither blaspheme nor misuse the name of God
by cursing,[1] perjury,[2] or unnecessary oaths,[3]
nor share in such horrible sins
by being silent bystanders.[4]

In a word, it requires
that we use the holy name of God
only with reverence and awe,[5]
so that we may properly
confess him,[6]
pray to him,[7]
and praise him in everything we do and say.[8]

[1]   Lev. 24:10-17

Now the son of an Israelite mother and an
Egyptian father went out among the Israelites,
and a fight broke out in the camp between him
and an Israelite. The son of the Israelite woman
blasphemed the Name with a curse; so they
brought him to Moses. (His mother's name was
Shelomith, the daughter of Dibri the Danite.)
They put him in custody until the will of the
Lord should be made clear to them.

Then the Lord said to Moses: "Take the blasphemer outside the camp. All those who heard
him are to lay their hands on his head, and the
entire assembly is to stone him. Say to the Israelites: 'If anyone curses his God, he will be
held responsible; anyone who blasphemes the
name of the Lord must be put to death. The entire assembly must stone him. Whether an alien
or native-born, when he blasphemes the Name,
he must be put to death.

" 'If anyone take the life of a human being, he
must be put to death.' "

[2]   Lev. 19:12

Do not swear falsely by my name and so
profane the name of your God. I am the Lord.

[3]   Matt. 5:37

Simply let your "Yes" be "Yes," and your
"No," "No"; anything beyond this comes from
the evil one.

James 5:12

Above all, my brothers, do not swear—not by
heaven or by earth or by anything else. Let your
"Yes" be yes, and your "No," no, or you will be
condemned.

[4]   Lev. 5:1

If a person sins because he does not speak up
when he hears a public charge to testify regarding something he has seen or learned about, he
will be held responsible.

Prov. 29:24

The accomplice of a thief is his own
enemy;
he is put under oath and dare not
testify;

[5]   Ps. 99:1-5

The Lord reigns,
let the nations tremble;
he sits enthroned between the cherubim,
let the earth shake.
Great is the Lord in Zion;
he is exalted over all the nations.
Let them praise your great and
awesome name—
he is holy.

The King is mighty, he loves justice—
you have established equity;
in Jacob you have done
what is just and right.
Exalt the Lord our God
and worship at his footstool;
he is holy.

Jer. 4:2

and if in a truthful, just and righteous way
you swear, "As surely as the Lord lives,"
then the nations will be blessed by him
and in him they will glory.

6   **Matt. 10:32-33**

Whoever acknowledges me before men, I will also acknowledge him before my Father in heaven. But whoever disowns me before men, I will disown him before my Father in heaven.

Rom. 10:9-10

That if you confess with your mouth, "Jesus is Lord," and believe in your heart that God raised him from the dead, you will be saved. For it is with your heart that you believe and are justified, and it is with your mouth that you confess and are saved.

7   **Ps. 50:14-15**

Sacrifice thank offerings to God,
    fulfill your vows to the Most High,
and call upon me in the day of trouble;
    I will deliver you, and you will
        honor me.

1 Tim. 2:8

I want men everywhere to lift up holy hands in prayer, without anger or disputing.

8   **Col. 3:17**

And whatever you do, whether in word or deed, do it all in the name of the Lord Jesus, giving thanks to God the Father through him.

100 Q. Is blasphemy of God's name by swearing and cursing
really such serious sin
that God is angry also with those
who do not do all they can
to help prevent it and forbid it?

    A. Yes, indeed.[1]
       No sin is greater,
       no sin makes God more angry
       than blaspheming his name.
    That is why he commanded the death penalty for it.[2]

1   **Lev. 5:1**

If a person sins because he does not speak up when he hears a public charge to testify regarding something he has seen or learned about, he will be held responsible.

2   **Lev. 24:10-17**

Now the son of an Israelite mother and an Egyptian father went out among the Israelites, and a fight broke out in the camp between him and an Israelite. The son of the Israelite woman blasphemed the Name with a curse; so they brought him to Moses. (His mother's name was Shelomith, the daughter of Dibri the Danite.) They put him in custody until the will of the LORD should be made clear to them.

Then the LORD said to Moses: "Take the blasphemer outside the camp. All those who heard him are to lay their hand on his head, and the entire assembly is to stone him. Say to the Israelites: 'If anyone curses his God, he will be held responsible; anyone who blasphemes the name of the LORD must be put to death. The entire assembly must stone him. Whether an alien or native-born, when he blasphemes the Name, he must be put to death.

" 'If anyone takes the life of a human being, he must be put to death.' "

**101 Q. But may we swear an oath in God's name
if we do it reverently?**

A. Yes, when the government demands it,
or when necessity requires it,
in order to maintain and promote truth and trustworthiness
for God's glory and our neighbor's good.

Such oaths are approved in God's Word[1]
and were rightly used by Old and New Testament believers.[2]

---

1 **Deut. 6:13**
Fear the LORD your God, serve him only and take your oaths in his name.

Deut. 10:20
Fear the LORD your God and serve him. Hold fast to him and take your oaths in his name.

Jer. 4:1-2
"If you will return, O Israel, return to me,"
declares the LORD.
"If you put your detestable idols out of
my sight
and no longer go astray,
and if in a truthful, just and righteous way
you swear, 'As surely as the LORD lives,'
then the nations will be blessed by him
and in him they will glory."

Heb. 6:16
Men swear by someone greater than themselves, and the oath confirms what is said and puts an end to all argument.

2 **Gen. 21:24**
Abraham said, "I swear it."

Josh. 9:15
Then Joshua made a treaty of peace with them to let them live, and the leaders of the assembly ratified it by oath.

1 Kings 1:29-30
The king then took an oath: "As surely as the LORD lives, who has delivered me out of every trouble, I will surely carry out today what I swore to you by the LORD, the God of Israel: Solomon your son shall be king after me, and he will sit on my throne in my place."

Rom. 1:9
God, whom I serve with my whole heart in preaching the gospel of his Son, is my witness how constantly I remember you.

2 Cor. 1:23
I call God as my witness that it was in order to spare you that I did not return to Corinth.

102 Q. May we swear by saints or other creatures?

A. No.
A legitimate oath means calling upon God
as the one who knows my heart
to witness to my truthfulness
and to punish me if I swear falsely.[1]
No creature is worthy of such honor.[2]

[1] **Rom. 9:1**

I speak the truth in Christ—I am not lying, my conscience confirms it in the Holy Spirit—

2 Cor. 1:23

I call God as my witness that it was in order to spare you that I did not return to Corinth.

[2] **Matt. 5:34-37**

But I tell you, Do not swear at all: either by heaven, for it is God's throne; or by the earth, for it is his footstool; or by Jerusalem, for it is the city of the Great King. And do not swear by your head, for you cannot make even one hair white or black. Simply let your "Yes" be "Yes," and your "No," "No"; anything beyond this comes from the evil one.

Matt. 23:16-22

Woe to you, blind guides! You say, "If anyone swears by the temple, it means nothing; but if anyone swears by the gold of the temple, he is bound by his oath." You blind fools! Which is greater: the gold, or the temple that makes the gold sacred? You also say, "If anyone swears by the altar, it means nothing; but if anyone swears by the gift on it, he is bound by his oath." You blind men! Which is greater: the gift, or the altar that makes the gift sacred? Therefore, he who swears by the altar swears by it and by everything on it. And he who swears by the temple swears by it and by the one who dwells in it. And he who swears by heaven swears by God's throne and by the one who sits on it.

James 5:12

Above all, my brothers, do not swear—not by heaven or by earth or by anything else. Let your "Yes" be yes, and your "No," no, or you will be condemned.

103 Q. **What is God's will for you**
in the fourth commandment?

A. First,
that the gospel ministry and education for it be maintained,[1]
and that, especially on the festive day of rest,
I regularly attend the assembly of God's people[2]
to learn what God's Word teaches,[3]
to participate in the sacraments,[4]
to pray to God publicly,[5]
and to bring Christian offerings for the poor.[6]

Second,
that every day of my life
I rest from my evil ways,
let the Lord work in me through his Spirit,
and so begin already in this life
the eternal Sabbath.[7]

1   **Deut. 6:4-9**

Hear, O Israel: The LORD our God, the LORD is one. Love the LORD your God with all your heart and with all your soul and with all your strength. These commandments that I give you today are to be upon your hearts. Impress them on your children. Talk about them when you sit at home and when you walk along the road, when you lie down and when you get up. Tie them as symbols on your hands and bind them on your foreheads. Write them on the doorframes of your houses and on your gates.

Deut. 6:20-25

In the future, when your son asks you, "What is the meaning of the stipulations, decrees and laws the LORD our God has commanded you?" tell him: "We were slaves of Pharaoh in Egypt, but the LORD brought us out of Egypt with a mighty hand. Before our eyes the LORD sent miraculous signs and wonders—great and terrible—upon Eypt and Pharaoh and his whole household. But he brought us out from there to bring us in and give us the land that he promised on oath to our forefathers. The LORD commanded us to obey all these decrees and to fear the LORD our God, so that we might always prosper and be kept alive, as is the case today. And if we are careful to obey all this law before the LORD our God, as he has commanded us, that will be our righteousness."

1 Cor. 9:13-14

Don't you know that those who work in the temple get their food from the temple, and those who serve at the altar share in what is offered on the altar? In the same way, the LORD has commanded that those who preach the gospel should receive their living from the gospel.

2 Tim. 2:2

And the things you have heard me say in the presence of many witnesses entrust to reliable men who will also be qualified to teach others.

2 Tim. 3:13-17

while evil men and impostors will go from bad to worse, deceiving and being deceived. But as for you, continue in what you have learned and have become convinced of, because you know those from whom you learned it, and how from infancy you have known the holy Scriptures, which are able to make you wise for salvation through faith in Christ Jesus. All Scripture is God-breathed and is useful for teaching, rebuking, correction and training in righteousness, so that the man of God may be thoroughly equipped for every good work.

Titus 1:5

The reason I left you in Crete was that you might straighten out what was left unfinished and appoint elders in every town, as I directed you.

140

But you are to seek the place the LORD your God will choose from among all your tribes to put his Name there for his dwelling. To that place you must go; there bring your burnt offerings and sacrifices, your tithes and special gifts, what you have vowed to give and your freewill offerings, and the firstborn of your herds and flocks. There, in the presence of the LORD your God, you and your families shall eat and shall rejoice in everything you have put your hand to, because the LORD your God has blessed you.

You are not to do as we do here today, everyone as he sees fit, since you have not yet reached the resting place and the inheritance the LORD your God is giving you. But you will cross the Jordan and settle in the land the LORD your God is giving you as an inheritance, and he will give you rest from all your enemies around you so that you will live in safety. Then to the place the LORD your God will choose as a dwelling for his Name—there you are to bring everything I command you: your burnt offerings and sacrifices, your tithes and special gifts, and all the choice possessions you have vowed in the LORD. And there rejoice before the LORD your God, you, your sons and daughters, your menservants and maidservants, and the Levites from your towns, who have no allotment or inheritance of their own.

Ps. 40:9-10

I proclaim righteousness in the great assembly;
   I do not seal my lips,
      as you know, O LORD.
I do not hide you righteousness in my heart;
   I speak of your faithfulness and salvation.
I do not conceal your love and your truth
   from the great assembly.

Ps. 68:26

Praise God in the great congregation;
   praise the LORD in the assembly of
      Israel.

Acts 2:42-47

They devoted themselves to the apostles' teaching and to the fellowship, to the breaking of bread and to prayer. Everyone was filled with awe, and many wonders and miraculous signs were done by the apostles. All the believers were together and had everything in common. Selling their possessions and goods, they gave to anyone as he had need. Every day they continued to meet together in the temple courts. They broke bread in their homes and ate together with glad and sincere hearts, praising God and enjoying the favor of all the people. And the Lord added to their number daily those who were being saved.

Heb. 10:23-25

Let us hold unswervingly to the hope we profess, for he who promised is faithful. And let us consider how we may spur one another on toward love and good deeds. Let us not give up meeting together, as some are in the habit of doing, but let us encourage one another—and all the more as you see the Day approaching.

3   Rom. 10:14-17

How, then, can they call on the one they have not believed in? And how can they believe in the one of whom they have not heard? And how can they hear without someone preaching to them? And how can they preach unless they are sent? As it is written, "How beautiful are the feet of those who bring good news!"

But not all the Israelites accepted the good news. For Isaiah says, "Lord, who has believed our message?" Consequently, faith comes from hearing the message, and the message is heard through the word of Christ.

1 Cor. 14:31-32

For you can all prophesy in turn so that everyone may be instructed and encouraged. The spirits of prophets are subject to the control of prophets.

1 Tim. 4:13

Unti I come, devote yourself to the public reading of Scripture, to preaching and to teaching.

4   1 Cor. 11:23-25

For I received from the Lord what I also passed on to you: The Lord Jesus, on the night he was betrayed, took bread, and when he had given thanks, he broke it and said, "This is my body, which is for you; do this in remembrance of me." In the same way, after supper he took the cup, saying, "This cup is the new covenant in my blood; do this, whenever you drink it, in remembrance of me."

5   Col. 3:16

Let the word of Christ dwell in you richly as you teach and admonish one another with all wisdom, and as you sing psalms, hymns and spiritual songs with gratitude in your hearts to God.

1 Tim. 2:1

I urge, then, first of all, that requests, prayers, intercession and thanksgiving be made for everyone—

6   Ps. 50:14

Sacrifice thank offerings to God,
   fulfill your vows to the Most High . . . .

1 Cor. 16:2

On the first day of every week, each one of you should set aside a sum of money in keeping with his income, saving it up, so that when I come no collections will have to be made.

2 Cor. 8 and 9

And now, brothers, we want you to know about the grace that God has given the Macedonian churches. Out of the most severe trial, their overflowing joy and their extreme poverty welled up in rich generosity. For I testify that they gave as much as they were able, and even beyond their ability. Entirely on their own, they urgently pleaded with us for the privilege of sharing in this service to the saints. And they did not do as we expected, but they gave themselves first to the Lord and then to us in keeping with God's will. So we urged Titus, since he had earlier made a beginning, to bring also to completion this act of grace on your part. But just as you excel in everything—in faith, in speech, in knowledge, in complete earnestness and in your love for us—see that you also excel in this grace of giving.

I am not commanding you, but I want to test the sincerity of your love by comparing it with the earnestness of others. For you know the grace of our Lord Jesus Christ, that though he was rich, yet for your sakes he became poor, so that you through his poverty might become rich.

And here is my advice about what is best for you in this matter: Last year you were the first not only to give but also to have the desire to do so. Now finish the work, so that your eager willingness to do it may be matched by your completion of it, according to your means. For if the willingness is there, the gift is acceptable according to what one has, not according to what he does not have.

Our desire is not that others might be relieved while you are hard pressed, but that there might be equality. At the present time your plenty will supply what they need, so that in turn their plenty will supply what you need. Then there will be equality, as it is written: "He who gathered much did not have too much, and he who gathered little did not have too little."

I thank God, who put into the heart of Titus the same concern I have for you. For Titus not only welcomed our appeal, but he is coming to you with much enthusiasm and on his own initiative. And we are sending along with him the brother who is praised by all the churches for his service to the gospel. What is more, he was chosen by the churches to accompany us as we carry the offering, which we administer in order to honor the Lord himself and to show our eagerness to help. We want to avoid any criticism of the way we administer this liberal gift. For we are taking pains to do what is right, not only in the eyes of the Lord but also in the eyes of men.

In addition, we are sending with them our brother who has often proved to us in many ways that he is zealous, and now even more so because of his great confidence in you. As for Titus, he is my partner and fellow worker among you; as for our brothers, they are representatives of the churches and an honor to Christ. Therefore show these men the proof of your love and the reason for our pride in you, so that the churches can see it.

There is no need for me to write to you about this service to the saints. For I know your eagerness to help, and I have been boasting about it to the Macedonians, telling them that since last year you in Achaia were ready to give; and your enthusiasm has stirred most of them to action. But I am sending the brothers in order that our boasting about you in this matter should not prove hollow, but that you may be ready, as I said you would be. For if any Macedonians come with me and find you unprepared, we—not to say anything about you—would be ashamed of having been so confident. So I thought it necessary to urge the brothers to visit you in advance and finish the arrangements for the generous gift you had promised. Then it will be ready as a generous gift, not as one grudgingly given.

Remember this: Whoever sows sparingly will also reap sparingly, and whoever sows generously will also reap generously. Each man should give what he has decided in his heart to give, not reluctantly or under compulsion, for God loves a cheerful giver. And God is able to make all grace abound to you, so that in all things at all times, having all that you need, you will abound in every good work. As it is written:

"He has scattered abroad his gifts to
    the poor;
his righteousness endures forever."

Now he who supplies seed to the sower and bread for food will also supply and increase your store of seed and will enlarge the harvest of your righteousness. You will be made rich in every way so that you can be generous on every occasion, and through us your generosity will result in thanksgiving to God.

This service that you perform is not only sup-plying the needs of God's people but is also over-flowing in many expressions of thanks to God. Because of the service by which you have proved yourselves, men will praise God for the obedience that accompanies your confession of the gospel of Christ, and for your generosity in sharing with them and with everyone else. And in their prayers for you their hearts will go out to you, because of the surpassing grace God has given you. Thanks be to God for his in-describable gift!

7   **Isa. 66:23**

"From one New Moon to another and from one Sabbath to another, all mankind will come and bow down before me," says the LORD.

Heb. 4:9-11

There remains, then, a Sabbath-rest for the people of God; for anyone who enters God's rest also rests from his own work, just as God did from his. Let us, therefore, make every effort to enter that rest, so that no one will fall by follow-ing their example of disboedience.

**104 Q. What is God's will for you
in the fifth commandment?**

A. That I honor, love, and be loyal to
my father and mother
and all those in authority over me;
that I obey and submit to them, as is proper,
when they correct and punish me;[1]
and also that I be patient with their failings—[2]
for through them God chooses to rule us.[3]

[1]   **Ex. 21:17**
Anyone who curses his father or mother must
be put to death.

Prov. 1:8
Listen, my son, to your father's instruction
and do not forsake your mother's teaching.

Prov. 4:1
Listen, my sons, to a father's instruction;
pay attention and gain understanding.

Rom. 13:1-2
Everyone must submit himself to the governing authorities, for there is no authority except
that which God established. The authorities that
exist have been established by God. Consequently, he who rebels against the authority is rebel-
ling against what God has instituted, and those
who do so will bring judgment on themselves.

Eph. 5:21-22
Submit to one another out of reverence for
Christ.
Wives, submit to your husbands as to the
Lord.

Eph. 6:1-9
Children, obey your parents in the Lord, for
this is right. "Honor your father and mother"—
which is the first commandment with a
promise—"that it may go well with you and that
you may enjoy life on the earth."
Fathers, do not exasperate your children; instead, bring them up in the training and instruction of the Lord.

Slaves, obey your earthly masters with respect
and fear, and with sincerity of heart, just as you
would obey Christ. Obey them not only to win
their favor when their eye is on you, but like
slaves of Christ, doing the will of God from your
heart. Serve wholeheartedly, as if you were serving the Lord, not men, because you know that
the Lord will reward everyone for whatever
good he does, whether he is slave or free.
And masters, treat your slaves in the same
way. Do not threaten them, since you know that
he who is both their Master and yours is in
heaven, and there is no favoritism with him.

Col. 3:18-4:1
Wives, submit to your husbands, as is fitting
in the Lord.
Husbands, love your wives and do not be
harsh with them.
Children, obey your parents in everything, for
this pleases the Lord.
Fathers, do not embitter your children, or they
will become discouraged.
Slaves, obey your earthly masters in everything; and do it, not only when their eye is on
you and to win their favor, but with sincerity of
heart and reverence for the Lord. Whatever you
do, work at it with all your heart, as working for
the Lord, not for men, since you know that you
will receive an inheritance from the Lord as a
reward. It is the Lord Christ you are serving.
Anyone who does wrong will be repaid for his
wrong, and there is no favoritism.
Masters, provide your slaves with what is
right and fair, because you know that you also
have a Master in heaven.

2

Prov. 20:20

If a man curses his father or mother,
his lamp will be snuffed out in pitch
darkness.

Prov. 23:22

Listen to your father, who gave you life,
and do not despise your mother
when she is old.

1 Pet. 2:18

Slaves, submit yourselves to your masters
with all respect, not only to those who are good
and considerate, but also to those who are harsh.

3

Matt. 22:21

"Caesar's," they replied.
Then he said to them, "Give to Caesar what is
Caesar's, and to God what is God's."

Rom. 13:1-8

Everyone must submit himself to the governing authorities, for there is no authority except
that which God has established. The authorities
that exist have been established by God. Consequently, he who rebels against the authority is re-
belling against what God has instituted, and
those who do so will bring judgment on themselves. For rulers hold no terror for those who do
right, but for those who do wrong. Do you want
to be free from fear of the one in authority? Then
do what is right and he will commend you. For
he is God's servant to do you good. But if you do
wrong, be afraid, for he does not bear the sword
for nothing. He is God's servant, an agent of
wrath to bring punishment on the wrongdoer.
Therefore, it is necessary to submit to the
authorities, not only because of possible punishment but also because of conscience.

This is also why you pay taxes, for the
authorities are God's servants, who give their
full time to governing. Give everyone what you
owe him: If you owe taxes, pay taxes; if revenue,
then revenue; if respect, then respect; if honor,
then honor.

Let no debt remain outstanding, except the
continuing debt to love one another, for he who
loves his fellowman has fulfilled the law.

Eph. 6:1-9

(Cf. footnote 1.)

Col. 3:18-21

(Cf. footnote 1.)

105 Q. **What is God's will for you**
in the sixth commandment?

A. I am not to belittle, insult, hate, or kill my neighbor—
not by my thoughts, my words, my look or gesture,
and certainly not by actual deeds—
and I am not to be party to this in others;[1]
rather, I am to put away all desire for revenge.[2]

I am not to harm or recklessly endanger myself either.[3]

Prevention of murder is also why
government is armed with the sword.[4]

[1] **Gen. 9:6**

"Whoever sheds the blood of man,
by man shall his blood be shed;
for in the image of God
has God made man.

Lev. 19:17-18

Do not hate your brother in your heart.
Rebuke your neighbor frankly so you will not
share in his guilt.
Do not seek revenge or bear a grudge against
one of your people, but love your neighbor as
yourself. I am the Lord.

Matt. 5:21-22

You have heard that it was said to the people
long ago, "Do not murder, and anyone who mur-
ders will be subject to judgment." But I tell you
that anyone who is angry with his brother will
be subject to judgment. Again, anyone who says
to his brother, "Raca," is answerable to the San-
hedrin. But anyone who says, "You fool!" will be
in danger of the fire of hell.

Matt. 26:52

"Put your sword back in its place," Jesus said
to him, "for all who draw the sword will die by
the sword."

[2] **Prov. 25:21-22**

If your enemy is hungry, give him food to eat;
if he is thirsty, give him water to drink.
In doing this, you will heap burning
coals on his head,
and the Lord will reward you.

Matt. 18:35

This is how my heavenly Father will meet each
of you unless you forgive your brother from
your heart.

Rom. 12:19

Do not take revenge, my friends, but leave
room for God's wrath, for it is written: "It is
mine to avenge; I will repay," says the Lord.

Eph. 4:26

"In your anger do not sin": Do not let the sun
go down while you are still angry . . . .

[3] **Matt. 4:7**

Jesus answered him, "It is also written: 'Do
not put the Lord your God to the test.' "

Matt. 26:52

"Put your sword back in its place," Jesus said
to him, "for all who draw the sword will die by
the sword."

Rom. 13:11-14

And do this, understanding the present time.
The hour has come for you to wake up from
your slumber, because our salvation is nearer
now than when we first believed. The night is
nearly over; the day is almost here. So let us put
aside the deeds of darkness and put on the
armor of light. Let us behave decently, as in the
daytime, not in orgies and drunkenness, not in
sexual immorality and debauchery, not in dissen-
sion and jealousy. Rather, clothe yourselves with
the Lord Jesus Christ, and do not think about
how to gratify the desires of the sinful nature.

[4] **Gen. 9:6**

Whoever sheds the blood of man,
by man shall his blood be shed;
for in the image of God
has God made man.

Ex. 21:14

But if a man schemes and kills another man deliberately, take him away from my altar and put him to death.

Rom. 13:4

For he is God's servant to do you good. But if you do wrong, be afraid, for he does not bear the sword for nothing. He is God's servant, an agent of wrath to bring punishment on the wrongdoer.

106 Q. Does this commandment refer only to killing?

A. By forbidding murder God teaches us
that he hates the root of murder:
envy, hatred, anger, vindictiveness.[1]

In God's sight all such are murder.[2]

[1] **Prov. 14:30**
A heart at peace gives life to the body,
but envy rots the bones.

Rom. 1:29
They have become filled with every kind of wickedness, evil, greed and depravity. They are full of envy, murder, strife, deceit and malice. They are gossips.

Rom. 12:19
Do not take revenge, my friends, but leave room for God's wrath, for it is written: "It is mine to avenge; I will repay," says the Lord.

Gal. 5:19-21
The acts of the sinful nature are obvious: sexual immorality, impurity and debauchery; idolatry and witchcraft; hatred, discord, jealousy, fits of rage, selfish ambition, dissensions, factions and envy; drunkenness, orgies, and the like. I warn you, as I did before, that those who live like this will not inherit the kingdom of God.

1 John 2:9-11
Anyone who claims to be in the light but hates his brother is still in the darkness. Whoever loves his brother lives in the light, and there is nothing in him to make him stumble. But whoever hates his brother is in the darkness and walks around in the darkness; he does not know where he is going, because the darkness has blinded him.

[2] **1 John 3:15**
Anyone who hates his brother is a murderer, and you know that no murderer has eternal life in him.

107 Q. Is it enough then
that we do not kill our neighbor
in any such way?

A. No.
By condemning envy, hatred, and anger
God tells us
to love our neighbors as ourselves,[1]
to be patient, peace-loving, gentle,
merciful, and friendly to them,[2]
to protect them from harm as much as we can,
and to do good even to our enemies.[3]

[1]   **Matt. 7:12**
So in everything, do to others what you
would have them do to you, for this sums up the
Law and the Prophets.

Matt. 22:39
And the second is like it: "Love your neighbor
as yourself."

Rom. 12:10
Be devoted to one another in brotherly love.
Honor one another above yourselves.

[2]   **Matt. 5:3-12**
Blessed are the poor in spirit,
for theirs is the kingdom of heaven.
Blessed are those who mourn,
for they will be comforted.
Blessed are the meek,
for they will inherit the earth.
Blessed are those who hunger and thirst
for righteousness.
for they will be filled.
Blessed are the merciful,
for they will be shown mercy.
Blessed are the pure in heart,
for they will see God.
Blessed are the peacemakers,
for they will be called sons of God.
Blessed are those who are persecuted
because of righteousness,
for theirs is the kingdom of heaven.
Blessed are you when people insult you, persecute you and falsely say all kinds of evil
against you because of me. Rejoice and be glad,
because great is your reward in heaven, for in
the same way they persecuted the prophets who
were before you.

Luke 6:36
Be merciful, just as your Father is merciful.

Rom. 12:10, 18
Be devoted to one another in brotherly love.
Honor one another in brotherly love. Honor one
another above yourselves.
If it is possible, as far as it depends on you,
live at peace with everyone.

Gal. 6:1-2
Brothers, if someone is caught in a sin, you
who are spiritual should restore him gently. But
watch yourself, or you also may be tempted.
Carry each other's burdens, and in this way you
will fulfill the law of Christ.

Eph. 4:2
Be completely humble and gentle; be patient,
bearing with one another in love.

Col. 3:12
Therefore, as God's chosen people, holy and
dearly loved, clothes yourselves with compassion, kindness, humility, gentleness and patience.

1 Pet. 3:8
Finally, all of you, live in harmony with one
another; be sympathetic, love as brothers, be
compassionate and humble.

[3]   **Ex. 23:4-5**
If you come across your enemy's ox or
donkey wandering off, be sure to take it back to
him. If you see the donkey of someone who
hates you fallen down under its load, do not
leave it there; be sure you help him with it.

Matt. 5:44-45
But I tell you: Love your enemies and pray for
those who persecute you, that you may be sons
of your Father in heaven. He causes his sun to
rise on the evil and the good, and sends rain on
the righteous and the unrighteous.

Rom. 12:20-21 (Prov. 25:21-22)

On the contrary:

"It your enemy is hungry, feed him;
    if he is thirsty, give him something to drink.
In doing this, you will heap burning
        coals on his head."

Do not be overcome by evil, but overcome evil
with good.

**108 Q. What is God's will for us
in the seventh commandment?**

A. God condemns all unchastity.[1]
We should therefore thoroughly detest it[2]
and, married or single,
live decent and chaste lives.[3]

1   Lev. 18:30

Keep my requirements and do not follow any of the detestable customs that were practiced before you came and do not defile yourselves with them. I am the LORD your God.

Eph. 5:3-5

But among you there must not be even a hint of sexual immorality, or of any kind of impurity, or of greed, because these are improper for God's holy people. Nor should there be obscenity, foolish talk or coarse joking, which are out of place, but rather thanksgiving. For of this you can be sure: No immoral, impure or greedy person—such a man is an idolater—has any inheritance in the kingdom of Christ and of God.

2   Jude 22-23

Be merciful to those who doubt; snatch others from the fire and save them; to others show mercy, mixed with fear—hating even the clothing stained by corrupted flesh.

3   1 Cor. 7:1-9

Now for the matters you wrote about: It is good for a man not to marry. But since there is so much immorality, each man should have his own wife, and each woman her own husband. The husband should fulfill his marital duty to his wife, and likewise the wife to her husband. The wife's body does not belong to her alone but also to her husband. In the same way, the husband's body does not belong to him alone but also to his wife. Do not deprive each other except by mutual consent and for a time, so that you may devote yourselves to prayer. Then come together again so that Satan will not tempt you because of your lack of self-control. I say this as a concession, not as a command. I wish that all men were as I am. But each man has his own gift from God; one has this gift, another has that.

Now to the unmarried and the widows I say: It is good for them to stay unmarried, as I am. But if they cannot control themselves, they should marry, for it is better to marry than to burn with passion.

1 Thess. 4:3-8

It is God's will that you should be sanctified: that you should avoid sexual immorality; that each of you should learn to control his own body in a way that is holy and honorable, not in passionate lust like the heathen, who do not know God; and that in this matter no one should wrong his brother or take advantage of him. The Lord will punish men for all such sins, as we have already told you and warned you. For God did not call us to be impure, but to live a holy life. Therefore, he who rejects this instruction does not reject man but God, who gives you his Holy Spirit.

Heb. 13:4

Marriage should be honored by all, and the marriage bed kept pure, for God will judge the adulterer and all the sexually immoral.

109 Q. Does God, in this commandment,
forbid only such scandalous sins as adultery?

A. We are temples of the Holy Spirit, body and soul,
and God wants both to be kept clean and holy.
That is why he forbids
everything which incites unchastity,[1]
whether it be actions, looks, talk, thoughts, or desires.[2]

1   1 Cor. 15:33

Do not be misled: "Bad company corrupts
good character."

Eph. 5:18

Do not get drunk on wine, which leads to
debauchery. Instead, be filled with the Spirit.

2   Matt. 5:27-29

You have heard that it was said, "Do not commit adultery." But I tell you that anyone who
looks at a woman lustfully has already committed adultery with her in his heart. If your
right eye causes you to sin, gouge it out, and
throw it away. It is better for you to lose one part
of your body than for your whole body to be
thrown into hell.

1 Cor. 6:18-20

Flee from sexual immorality. All other sins a
man commits are outside his body, but he who
sins sexually sins against his own body. Do you
not know that your body is a temple of the Holy
Spirit, who is in you, whom you have received
from God? You are not your own; you were
bought at a price. Therefore honor God with
your body.

Eph. 5:3-4

But among you there must not be even a hint
of sexual immorality, or of any kind of impurity,
or of greed, because these are improper for
God's holy people. Nor should there be
obscenity, foolish talk or course joking, which are
out of place, but rather thanksgiving.

**110 Q. What does God forbid
in the eighth commandment?**

A. He forbids not only outright theft and robbery,
punishable by law.[1]

But in God's sight theft also includes
cheating and swindling our neighbor
by schemes made to appear legitimate,[2]
such as:
inaccurate measurements of weight, size, or volume;
fraudulent merchandising;
counterfeit money;
excessive interest;
or any other means forbidden by God.[3]

In addition he forbids all greed[4]
and pointless squandering of his gifts.[5]

---

1   Ex. 22:1

"If a man steals an ox or a sheep and slaughters it or sells it, he must pay back five head of cattle for the ox and four sheep for the sheep.

1 Cor. 5:9-10

I have written you in my letter not to associate with sexually immoral people—not at all meaning the people of this world who are immoral, or the greedy and swindlers, or idolaters. In that case you would have to leave this world.

1 Cor. 6:9-10

Do you not know that the wicked will not inherit the kingdom of God? Do not be deceived: Neither the sexually immoral nor idolaters nor adulterers nor male prostitutes not homosexual offenders nor thieves nor the greedy nor drunkards nor slanderers nor swindlers will inherit the kingdom of God.

2   Mic. 6:9-11

Listen! The Lord is calling to the city—
and to fear your name is wisdom—
"Heed the rod and the One who
appointed it.
Am I still to forget, O wicked house,
your ill-gotten treasures
and the short ephah, which is accursed?
Shall I acquit a man with dishonest scales,
with a bag of false weights?"

Luke 3:14

Then some soldiers asked him, "And what should we do?"
He replied, "Don't extort money and don't accuse people falsely—be content with your pay."

James 5:1-6

Now listen, you rich people, weep and wail because of the misery that is coming upon you. Your wealth has rotted, and moths have eaten your clothes. Your gold and silver are corroded. Their corrosion will testify against you and eat your flesh like fire. You have hoarded wealth in the last days. Look! The wages you failed to pay the workmen who mowed your fields are crying out against you. The cries of the harvesters have reached the ears of the Lord Almighty. You have lived on earth in luxury and self-indulgence. You have fattened yourselves in the day of slaughter. You have condemned and murdered innocent men, who were not opposing you.

3   Deut. 25:13-16

Do not have two differing weights in your bag—one heavy, one light. Do not have two differing measures in your house—one large, one small. You must have accurate and honest weights and measures, so that you may live long in the land the Lord your God is giving you. For the Lord your God detests anyone who does these things, anyone who deals dishonestly.

Psalm 15:5

who lends his money without usury
and does not accept a bribe against
the innocent.

Prov. 11:1

The Lord abhors dishonest scales,
but accurate weights are his delight.

Prov. 12:22

The Lord detests lying lips,
but he delights in men who are truthful.

Ezek. 45:9-12

This is what the Sovereign Lord says: You have gone far enough, O princes of Israel! Give up your violence and oppression and do what is just and right. Stop dispossessing my people, declares the Sovereign Lord. You are to use accurate scales, an accurate ephah and an accurate bath. The ephah and the bath are to be the same size, the bath containing a tenth of a homer and the ephah a tenth of a homer; the homer is to be the standard measure for both. The shekel is to consist of twenty gerahs. Twenty shekels plus twenty-five shekels plus fifteen shekels equal one mina.

Luke 6:35

But love your enemies, do good to them, and lend to them without expecting to get anything back. Then your reward will be great, and you will be sons of the Most High, because he is kind to the ungrateful and wicked.

4 ### Luke 12:15

Then he said to them, "Watch out! Be on your guard against all kinds of greed; a man's life does not consist in the abundance of his possessions."

Eph. 5:5

For of this you can be sure: No immoral, impure or greedy person—such a man is an idolater—has any inheritance in the kingdom of Christ and of God.

5 ### Prov. 21:20

In the house of the wise are stores of
choice food and oil,
but a foolish man devours all he has.

Prov. 23:20-21

Do not join those who drink too much wine
or gorge themselves on meat,
for drunkards and gluttons become poor,
and drowsiness clothes them in rags.

Luke 16:10-13

Whoever can be trusted with very little can also be trusted with much, and whoever is dishonest with very little will also be dishonest with much. So if you have not been trustworthy in handling worldly wealth, who will trust you with true riches? And if you have not been trustworthy with someone else's property, who will give you property of your own?

No servant can serve two masters. Either he will hate the one and love the other, or he will be devoted to the one and despise the other. You cannot serve both God and Money.

**111 Q. What does God require of you
in this commandment?**

    A. That I do whatever I can
        for my neighbor's good,
    that I treat others
        as I would like them to treat me,
    and that I work faithfully
        so that I may share with those in need.[1]

---

1   **Isa. 58:5-10**

Is this the kind of fast I have chosen,
   only a day for a man to humble himself?
Is it only for bowing one's head like a reed
   and for lying on sackcloth and ashes?
Is that what you call a fast,
   a day acceptable to the Lord?

Is not this the kind of fasting I have chosen:
 to loose the chains of injustice
   and untie the cords of the yoke,
to set the oppressed free
   and break every yoke?
Is it not to share your food with the hungry
   and to provide the poor wanderer
      with shelter—
when you see the naked, to clothe him,
   and not to turn away from your own
      flesh and blood?
Then your light will break forth like the dawn,
   and your healing will quickly appear;
then your righteousness will go before you,
   and the glory of the Lord will be
      your rear guard.
Then you will call, and the Lord will answer;
   you will cry for help, and he will say:
      Here am I.

If you do away with the yoke of oppression,
   with the pointing finger and malicious talk,
and if you spend yourselves in behalf of
      the hungry
   and satisfy the needs of the oppressed,
then your light will rise in the darkness,
   and your night will become like the noonday.

Matt. 7:12

So in everything, do to others what you
would have them do to you, for this sums up the
Law and the Prophets.

Gal. 6:9-10

Let us not become weary in doing good, for at
the proper time we will reap a harvest if we do
not give up. Therefore, as we have opportunity,
let us do good to all people, especially to those
who belong to the family of believers.

Eph. 4:28

He who has been stealing must steal no
longer, but must work, doing something useful
with his own hands, that he may have something to share with those in need.

**112 Q. What is God's will for you
in the ninth commandment?**

A. God's will is that I
never give false testimony against anyone,
twist no one's words,
not gossip or slander,
nor join in condemning anyone
without a hearing or without a just cause.[1]

Rather, in court and everywhere else,
I should avoid lying and deceit of every kind;
these are devices the devil himself uses,
and they would call down on me God's intense anger.[2]
I should love the truth,
speak it candidly,
and openly acknowledge it.[3]
And I should do what I can
to guard and advance my neighbor's good name.[4]

---

1   **Ps. 15**

LORD, who may dwell in your sanctuary?
Who may live on your holy hill?

He whose walk is blameless
and who does what is righteous,
who speaks the truth from his heart
and has no slander on his tongue,
who does his neighbor no wrong
and casts no slur on his fellow man,
who despises a vile man
but honors those who fear the LORD,
who keeps his oath
even when it hurts,
who lends his money without usury
and does not accept a bribe against
the innocent.
He who does these things
will never be shaken.

Prov. 19:5

A false witness will not go unpunished,
and he who pours out lies will not go free.

Matt. 7:1

Do not judge, or you too will be judged.

Luke 6:37

Do not judge, and you will not be judged. Do
not condemn, and you will not be condemned.
Forgive, and you will be forgiven.

Rom. 1:28-32

Furthermore, since they did not think it
worthwhile to retain the knowledge of God, he
gave them over to a depraved mind, to do what
ought not to be done. They have become filled
with every kind of wickedness, evil, greed and
depravity. They are full of envy, murder, strife,
deceit and malice. They are gossips, slanderers,
God-haters, insolent, arrogant and boastful; they
invent ways of doing evil; they disobey their
parents; they are senseless, faithless, heartless,
ruthless. Although they know God's righteous
decree that those who do such things deserve
death, they not only continue to do these very
things but also approve of those who practice
them.

2   **Lev. 19:11-12**

Do not steal.
Do not lie.
Do not deceive one another.
Do not swear falsely by my name and so profane
the name of your God. I am the LORD.

Prov. 12:22

The LORD detests lying lips,
but he delights in men who are truthful.

Prov. 13:5

The righteous hate what is false,
but the wicked bring shame and disgrace.

John 8:44

You belong to your father, the devil, and you want to carry out your father's desire. He was a murderer from the beginning, not holding to the truth, for there is no truth in him. When he lies, he speaks his native language, for he is a liar and the father of lies.

Rev. 21:8

But the cowardly, the unbelieving, the vile, the murderers, the sexually immoral, those who practice magic arts, the idolaters and all liars—their place will be in the fiery lake of burning sulfur. This is the second death.

3   **1 Cor. 13:6**

Love does not delight in evil but rejoices with the truth.

Eph. 4:25

Therefore each of you must put off falsehood and speak truthfully to his neighbor, for we are all members of one body.

4   **1 Pet. 3:8-9**

Finally, all of you, live in harmony with one another; be sympathetic, love as brothers, be compassionate and humble. Do not repay evil with evil or insult with insult, but with blessing, because to this you were called so that you may inherit a blessing.

1 Pet. 4:8

Above all, love each other deeply, because love covers over a multitude of sins.

**113 Q. What is God's will for you
in the tenth commandment?**

A. That not even the slightest thought or desire
contrary to any one of God's commandments
should ever arise in my heart.

Rather, with all my heart
I should always hate sin
and take pleasure in whatever is right.[1]

1   **Ps. 19:7-14**

The law of the LORD is perfect,
   reviving the soul.
The statutes of the LORD are trustworthy,
   making wise the simple.
The precepts of the LORD are right,
   giving joy to the heart.
The fear of the LORD is pure,
   enduring forever.
The ordinances of the Lord are sure
   and altogether righteous.
They are more precious than gold,
   than much pure gold;
they are sweeter than honey,
   than honesty from the comb.
By them is your servant warned;
   in keeping them there is great reward.

Who can discern his errors?
   Forgive my hidden faults.
Keep your servants also from willful sins;
   may they not rule over me.
Then will I be blameless,
   innocent of great transgression.

May the words of my mouth and the
       meditation of my heart
   be pleasing in your sight,
   O Lord, my Rock and my Redeemer.

Ps. 139:23-24

Search me, O God, and know my heart;
   test me and know my anxious thoughts.
See if there is any offensive way in me,
   and lead me in the way everlasting.

Rom. 7:7-8

What shall we say, then? Is the law sin? Certainly not! Indeed I would not have known what sin was except through the law. For I would not have known what coveting really was if the law had not said, "Do not covet." But sin, seizing the opportunity afforded by the commandment, produced in me every kind of covetous desire. For apart from law, sin is dead.

**114 Q. But can those converted to God
obey these commandments perfectly?**

A. No.
In this life even the holiest
have only a small beginning of this obedience.[1]

Nevertheless, with all seriousness of purpose,
they do begin to live
according to all, not only some,
of God's commandments.[2]

[1]   Eccl. 7:20
There is not a righteous man on earth
who does what is right and never sins.

Rom. 7:14-15
We know that the law is spiritual; but I am unspiritual, sold as a slave to sin. I do not understand what I do. For what I want to do I do not
do, but what I hate I do.

1 Cor. 13:9
For we know in part and we prophesy in
part . . . .

1 John 1:8-10
If we claim to be without sin, we deceive ourselves and the truth is not in us. If we confess
our sins, he is faithful and just and will forgive
us our sins and purify us from all unrighteousness. If we claim we have not sinned, we make
him out to be a liar and his word has no place in
our lives.

[2]   Ps. 1:1-2
Blessed is the man
who does not walk in the counsel
of the wicked
or stand in the way of sinners
or sit in the seat of mockers.
But his delight is in the law of the LORD,
and on his law he meditates day and night.

Rom. 7:22-25
For in my inner being I delight in God's law;
but I see another law at work in the members of
my body, waging war against the law of my
mind and making me a prisoner of the law of sin
at work within my members. What a wretched
man I am! Who will rescue me from this body of
death? Thanks be to God—through Jesus Christ
our Lord!
So then, I myself in my mind am a slave to
God's law, but in the sinful nature a slave to the
law of sin.

Phil. 3:12-16
Not that I have already obtained all this, or
have already been made perfect, but I press on to
take hold of that for which Christ Jesus took
hold of me. Brothers, I do not consider myself
yet to have taken hold of it. But one thing I do:
Forgetting what is behind and straining toward
what is ahead, I press on toward the goal to win
the prize for which God has called me heavenward in Christ Jesus.
All of us who are mature should take such a
view of things. And if on some point you think
differently, that too God will make clear to you.
Only let us live up to what we have already at-
tained.

115 Q. No one in this life
can obey the ten commandments perfectly:
why then does God want them
preached so pointedly?

A. First, so that the longer we live
the more we may come to know our sinfulness
and the more eagerly look to Christ
for forgiveness of sins and righteousness.[1]

Second, so that,
while praying to God for the grace of the Holy Spirit,
we may never stop striving
to be renewed more and more after God's image,
until after this life we reach our goal:
perfection.[2]

---

[1] **Ps. 32:5**

Then I acknowledged my sin to you
and did not cover up my iniquity.
I said, "I will confess
my transgressions to the LORD"—
and you forgave
the guilt of my sin.

Rom. 3:19-26

Now we know that whatever the law says, it says to those who are under the law, so that every mouth may be silenced and the whole world held accountable to God. Therefore no one will be declared righteous in his sight by observing the law; rather, through the law we become conscious of sin.

But now a righteousness from God, apart from law, has been made known, to which the Law and the Prophets testify. This righteousness from God comes through faith in Jesus Christ to all who believe. There is no difference, for all have sinned and fall short of the glory of God, and are justified freely by his grace through the redemption that came by Christ Jesus. God presented him as a sacrifice of atonement, through faith in his blood. He did this to demonstrate his justice, because in his forbearance he had left the sins committed beforehand unpunished— he did it to demonstrate his justice at the present time, so as to be just and the one who justifies those who have faith in Jesus.

Rom. 7:7, 24-25

What shall we say, then? Is the law sin? Certainly not! Indeed I would not have known what sin was except through the law. For I would not have known what coveting really was if the law had not said, "Do not covet."

What a wretched man I am! Who will rescue me from this body of death? Thanks be to God— through Jesus Christ our Lord!

So then, I myself in my mind am a slave to God's law, but in the sinful nature a slave to the law of sin.

1 John 1:9

If we confess our sins, he is faithful and just and will forgive us our sins and purify us from all unrighteousness.

[2] **1 Cor. 9:24**

Do you not know that in a race all the runners run, but only one gets the prize? Run in such a way as to get the prize.

Phil. 3:12-14

Not that I have already obtained all this, or have already been made perfect, but I press on to take hold of that for which Christ Jesus took hold of me.

Brothers, I do not consider myself yet to have taken hold of it. But one thing I do: Forgetting what is behind and straining toward what is ahead, I press on toward the goal to win the prize for which God has called me heavenward in Christ Jesus.

1 John 3:1-3

How great is the love the Father has lavished on us, that we should be called children of God! And that is what we are! The reason the world does not know us is that it did not know him. Dear friends, now we are children of God, and what we will be has not yet been made known. But we know that when he appears, we shall be like him, for we shall see him as he is. Everyone who has this hope in him purifies himself, just as he is pure.

LORD'S DAY 45

116 Q. Why do Christians need to pray?

A. Because prayer is the most important part
   of the thankfulness God requires of us.[1]
And also because God gives his grace and Holy Spirit
only to those who pray continually and groan inwardly,
   asking God for these gifts
   and thanking him for them.[2]

[1] **Ps. 50:14-15**
Sacrifice thank offerings to God,
   fulfill your vows to the Most High,
and call upon me in the day of trouble;
   I will deliver you, and you will honor me.

Ps. 116:12-19
How can I repay the Lord
   for all his goodness to me?
I will lift up the cup of salvation
   and call on the name of the Lord.
I will fulfill my vows to the Lord
   in the presence of all his people.

Precious in the sight of the Lord
   is the death of his saints.
O Lord, truly I am your servant;
   I am your servant, the son of your
      maidservant;
   you have freed me from my chains.

I will sacrifice a thank offering to you
   and call on the name of the Lord.
I will fulfill my vows to the Lord
   in the presence of all his people,
in the courts of the house of the Lord—
   in your midst, O Jerusalem.

Praise the Lord.

1 Thess. 5:16-18
Be joyful always; pray continually; give
thanks in all circumstances, for this is God's will
for you in Christ Jesus.

[2] **Matt. 7:7-8**
Ask and it will be given to you; seek and you
will find; knock and the door will be opened to
you. For everyone who asks receives; he who
seeks finds; and to him who knocks, the door
will be opened.

Luke 11:9-13
So I say to you: Ask and it will be given to
you; seek and you will find; knock and the door
will be opened to you. For everyone who asks
receives; he who seeks finds; and to him who
knocks, the door will be opened.

Which of you fathers, if your son asks for a
fish, will give him a snake instead? Or if he asks
for an egg, will give him a scorpion? If you then,
though you are evil, know how to give good
gifts to your children, how much more will your
Father in heaven give the Holy Spirit to those
who ask him!

117 Q. **How does God want us to pray**
so that he will listen to us?

A. First, we must pray from the heart
to no other than the one true God,
who has revealed himself in his Word,
asking for everything he has commanded us to ask for.[1]

Second, we must acknowledge our need and misery,
hiding nothing,
and humble ourselves in his majestic presence.[2]

Third, we must rest on this unshakable foundation:
even though we do not deserve it,
God will surely listen to our prayer
because of Christ our Lord.
That is what he promised us in his Word.[3]

1   Ps. 145:18-20

The Lord is near to all who call on him,
to all who call on him in truth.
He fulfills the desires of those who fear him;
he hears their cry and saves them.
The Lord watches over all who love him,
but all the wicked he will destroy.

John 4:22-24

You Samaritans worship what you do not
know; we worship what we do know, for salvation is from the Jews. Yet a time is coming and
has now come when the true worshipers will
worship the Father in spirit and truth, for they
are the kind of worshipers the Father seeks. God
is spirit, and his worshipers must worship in
spirit and in truth.

Rom. 8:26-27

In the same way, the Spirit helps us in our
weakness. We do not know what we ought to
pray for, but the Spirit himself intercedes for us
with groans that words cannot express. And he
who searches our hearts knows the mind of the
Spirit, because the Spirit intercedes for the saints
in accordance with God's will.

James 1:5

If any of you lacks wisdom, he should ask
God, who gives generously to all without find-
ing fault, and it will be given to him.

1 John 5:14-15

This is the confidence we have in approaching
God: that if we ask anything according to his
will, he hears us. And if we know that he hears
us—whatever we ask—we know that we have
what we asked of him.

2   2 Chron. 7:14

if my people, who are called by my name, will
humble themselves and pray and seek my face
and turn from their wicked ways, then will I
hear from heaven and will forgive their sin and
will heal their land.

Ps. 2:11

Serve the Lord with fear
and rejoice with trembling.
Kiss the Son, lest he be angry
and you be destroyed in your way,
for his wrath can flare up in a moment.
Blessed are all who take refuge in him.

Ps. 34:18

The Lord is close to the brokenhearted
and saves those who are crushed in spirit.

Ps. 62:8

Trust in him at all times, O people;
pour out your hearts to him,
for God is our refuge.

Isa. 66:2

"Has not my hand made all these things,
and so they came into being?"
declares the Lord.

"This is the one I esteem:
he who is humble and contrite in spirit,
and trembles at my word."

Rev. 4

After this I looked, and there before me was a
door standing open in heaven. And the voice I
had first heard speaking to me like a trumpet
said, "Come up here, and I will show you what
must take place after this." At once I was in the
Spirit, and there before me was a throne in
heaven with someone sitting on it. And the one

who sat there had the appearance of jasper and carnelian. A rainbow, resembling an emerald, encircled the throne. Surrounding the throne were twenty-four other thrones, and seated on them were twenty-four elders. They were dressed in white and had crowns of gold on their heads. From the throne came flashes of lightning, rumblings and peals of thunder. Before the throne, seven lamps were blazing. These are the seven spirits of God. Also before the throne there was what looked like a sea of glass, clear as crystal.

In the center, around the throne, were four living creatures, and they were covered with eyes, in front and in back. The first living creature was like a lion, the second was like an ox, the third had a face like a man, the fourth was like a flying eagle. Each of the four living creatures had six wings and was covered with eyes all around, even under his wings. Day and night they never stop saying:

"Holy, holy, holy
is the Lord God Almighty,
who was, and is, and is to come."

Whenever the living creatures give glory, honor and thanks to him who sits on the throne and who lives for ever and ever, the twenty-four elders fall down before him who sits on the throne, and worship him who lives for ever and ever. They lay their crowns before the throne and say:

"You are worthy, our Lord and God,
to receive glory and honor and power,
for you created all things,
and by your will they were created
and have their being."

3   ### Dan. 9:17-19

Now, our God, hears the prayers and petitions of your servant. For your sake, O Lord, look with favor on your desolate sanctuary. Give ear, O God, and hear; open your eyes and see the desolation of the city that bears your Name. We do not make requests of you because we are righteous, but because of your great mercy. O Lord, listen! O Lord, forgive! O Lord, hear and act! For your sake, O my God, do not delay, because your city and your people bear your Name.

Matt. 7:8

For everyone who asks receives; he who seeks finds; and to him who knocks, the door will be opened.

John 14:13-14

And I will do whatever you ask in my name, so that the Son may bring glory to the Father. You may ask me for anything in my name, and I will do it.

John 16:23

In that day, you will no longer ask me anything. I tell you the truth, my Father will give you whatever you ask in my name.

Rom. 10:13

Everyone who calls on the name of the Lord will be saved.

James 1:6

But when he asks, he must believe and not doubt, because he who doubts is like a wave of the sea, blown and tossed by the wind.

118 Q. What did God command us to pray for?

A. Everything we need, spiritually and physically,[1]
as embraced in the prayer
Christ our Lord taught us.

1   **James 1:17**

Every good and perfect gift is from above, coming down from the Father of the heavenly lights, who does not change like shifting shadows.

Matt. 6:33

But seek first his kingdom and his righteousness, and all these things will be given to you as well.

119 Q. What is this prayer?

    A. Our Father in heaven,
       hallowed be your name
       your kingdom come,
       your will be done
           on earth as it is in heaven.
       Give us today our daily bread.
       Forgive us our debts,
           as we also have forgiven our debtors.
       And lead us not into temptation,
           but deliver us from the evil one.
       For yours is the kingdom
          and the power
          and the glory forever.
       Amen.[1]*

1   **Matt. 6:9-13**

This, then, is how you should pray:

"Our Father in heaven,
hallowed by your name,
your kingdom come,
your will be done
   on earth as it is in heaven.
Give us today our daily bread.
 Forgive us our debts,
   as we also have forgiven our debtors.
 And lead us not into temptation,
but deliver us from the evil one."

Luke 11:2-4

He said to them, "When you pray, say:

" 'Father,
hallowed be your name,
your kingdom come.
Give us each day our daily bread.
Forgive us our sins,
   for we also forgive everyone who sins
      against us.

And lead us not into temptation.' "

*Earlier and better manuscripts of Matthew 6 omit the words "For yours is . . . Amen."

120 Q. Why did Christ command us
to call God "our Father"?

A. At the very beginning of our prayer
Christ wants to kindle in us
what is basic to our prayer—
the childlike awe and trust
that God through Christ has become
our Father.

Our fathers do not refuse us
the things of this life;
God our Father will even less refuse to give us
what we ask in faith.[1]

1 **Matt. 7:9-11**
Which of you, if his son asks for bread, will give him a stone? Or if he asks for a fish, will give him a snake? If you, then, though you are evil, know how to give good gifts to your children, how much more will your Father in heaven give good gifts to those who ask him!

Luke 11:11-13
Which of you fathers, if your son asks for a fish, will give him a snake instead? Or if he asks for an egg, will give him a scorpion? If you then, though you are evil, know how to give good gifts to your children, how much more will your Father in heaven give the Holy Spirit to those who ask him!

**121 Q. Why the words
"in heaven"?**

A. These words teach us
not to think of God's heavenly majesty
as something earthly,[1]
and to expect everything
for body and soul
from his almighty power.[2]

1 Jer. 23:23-24

"Am I only a God nearby,"
declares the Lord,
"and not a God far away?
Can anyone hide in secret places
so that I cannot see him?"
declares the Lord.
"Do not I fill heaven and earth?"
declares the Lord.

Acts 17:24-25

The God who made the world and everything in it is the Lord of heaven and earth and does not live in temples built by hands. And he is not served by human hands, as if he needed anything, because he himself gives all men life and breath and everything else. From one man he made every nation of men, that they should inhabit the whole earth; and he determined the times set for them and the exact places where they should live.

2 Matt. 6:25-34

"Therefore I tell you, do not worry about your life, what you will eat or drink; or about your body, what you will wear. Is not life more important than food, and the body more important than clothes? Look at the birds of the air; they do not sow or reap or store away in barns, and yet your heavenly Father feeds them. Are you not much more valuable than they? Who of you by worrying can add a single hour to his life?

"And why do you worry about clothes? See how the lilies of the field grow. They do not labor or spin. Yet I tell you that not even Solomon in all his splendor was dressed like one of these. If that is how God clothes the grass of the field, which is here today and tomorrow is thrown into the fire, will he not much more clothe you, O you of little faith? So do not worry, saying, 'What shall we eat?' or 'What shall we drink?' or 'What shall we wear?' For the pagans run after all these things, and your heavenly Father knows that you need them. But seek first his kingdom and his righteousness, and all these things will be given to you as well. Therefore do not worry about tomorrow, for tomorrow will worry about itself. Each day has enough trouble of its own.

Rom. 8:31-32

What, then, shall we say in response to this? If God is for us, who can be against us? He who did not spare his own Son, but gave him up for us all—how will he not also, along with him, graciously give us all things?

122 Q. What does the first request mean?

A. *Hallowed be your name* means,

Help us to really know you,[1]
to bless, worship, and praise you
for all your works
and for all that shines forth from them:
your almighty power, wisdom, kindness,
justice, mercy, and truth.[2]

And it means,

Help us to direct all our living—
what we think, say, and do—
so that your name will never be blasphemed because of us
but always honored and praised.[3]

[1] **Jer. 9:23-24**
This is what the Lord says:

"Let not the wise man boast of his wisdom
or the strong man boast of his strength
or the rich man boast of his riches,
but let him who boasts boast about this:
that he understands and knows me,
that I am the Lord, who exercises kindness,
justice and righteousness on earth,
for in these I delight,"
declares the Lord.

Jer. 31:33-34
"This is the covenant I will make with
the house of Israel
after that time," declares the Lord.

"I will put my law in their minds
and write it on their hearts.
I will be their God,
and they will be my people.
No longer will a man teach his neighbor,
or a man his brother, saying, 'Know
the Lord,'
because they will all know me,
from the least of them to the greatest,"
declares the Lord.
"For I will forgive their wickedness
and will remember their sins no more."

Matt. 16:17
Jesus replied, "Blessed are you, Simon son of
Jonah, for this was not revealed to you by man,
but by my Father in heaven."

John 17:3
Now this is eternal life: that they may know
you, the only true God, and Jesus Christ, whom
you have sent.

[2] **Ex. 34:5-8**
Then the Lord came down in the cloud and
stood there with him and proclaimed his name,
the Lord. And he passed in front of Moses,
proclaiming, "The Lord, the Lord, the compassionate and gracious God, slow to anger, abounding in love and faithfulness, maintaining love to
thousands, and forgiving wickedness, rebellion
and sin. Yet he does not leave the guilty unpunished; he punishes the children and their
children for the sin of the fathers to the third and
fourth generation."
Moses bowed to the ground at once and wor-
shiped.

Ps. 145
I will exalt you, my God the King;
I will praise your name for ever and ever.
Every day I will praise you
and extol your name for ever and ever.

Great is the Lord and most worthy of praise;
his greatness no one can fathom.
One generation will commend your
works to another;
they will tell of your mighty acts.
They will speak of the glorious
splendor of your majesty,
and I will meditate on your
wonderful works.
They will tell of the power of your

awesome works,
and I will proclaim your great deeds.
They will celebrate your abundant goodness
and joyfully sing of your righteousness.

The Lord is gracious and compassionate,
slow to anger and rich in love.
The Lord is good to all;
he has compassion on all he has made.
All you have made will praise you, O Lord;
your saints will extol you.

They will tell of the glory of your kingdom
and speak of your might,
so that all men may know of your mighty acts
and the glorious splendor of your kingdom.
Your kingdom is an everlasting kingdom,
and your dominion endures through
all generations.

The Lord is faithful to all his promises
and loving toward all he has made.
The Lord upholds all those who fall
and lifts up all who are bowed down.
The eyes of all look to you,
and you give them their food at the
proper time.
You open your hand
and satisfy the desires of every living thing.

The Lord is righteous in all his ways
and loving toward all he has made.
The Lord is near to all who call on him,
to all who call on him in truth
He fulfills the desires of those who fear him;
he hears their cry and saves them.
The Lord watches over all who love him,
but all the wicked he will destroy

My mouth will speak in praise of the Lord.
Let every creature praise his holy name
for ever and ever.

Jer. 32:16-20

After I had given the deed of purchase to
Baruch son of Neriah, I prayed to the Lord:

Ah, Sovereign Lord, you have made the
heavens and the earth by your great power and
outstretched arm. Nothing is too hard for you.
You show love to thousands but bring the
punishment for the fathers' sins into the laps of
their children after them. O great and powerful
God, whose name is the Lord Almighty, great are
your purposes and mighty are your deeds. Your
eyes are open to all the ways of men; you reward
everyone according to his conduct and as his
deeds deserve. You performed miraculous signs
and wonders in Egypt and have continued them
to this day, both in Israel and among all
mankind, and have gained the renown that is
still yours.

Luke 1:46-55

And Mary said:

"My soul glorifies the Lord
and my spirit rejoices in God my Savior,
for he has been mindful
of the humble state of his servant.
From now on all generations will call me blessed,
for the Mighty One has done great
things for me—
holy is his name.
His mercy extends to those who fear him,
from generation to generation.
He has performed mighty deeds with his arm;
he has scattered those who are proud
in their inmost thoughts.
He has brought down rulers from their thrones
but has lifted up the humble.
He has filled the hungry with good things
but has sent the rich away empty.
He has helped his servant Israel,
remembering to be merciful
to Abraham and his descendants forever,
even as he said to our fathers."

Luke 1:68-75

Praise be to the Lord, the God of Israel,
because he has come and has
redeemed his people.
He has raised up a horn of salvation for us
in the house of his servant David
(as he said through his holy prophets of
long ago),
salvation from our enemies
and from the hand of all who hate us—
to show mercy to our fathers
and to remember his holy covenant,
the oath he swore to our father Abraham:
to rescue us from the hand of our enemies,
and to enable us to serve him without fear
in holiness and righteousness before
him all our days.

Rom. 11:33-36

Oh, the depth of the riches of the
wisdom and knowledge of God!
How unsearchable his judgments,
and his paths beyond tracing out!
"Who has known the mind of the Lord?
Or who has been his counselor?"
"Who has ever given to God,
that God should repay him?"
For from him and through him and to
him are all things.
To him be the glory forever! Amen.

3 ### Ps. 115:1

Not to us, O Lord, not to us
but to your name be the glory,
because of your love and faithfulness.

Matt. 5:16

In the same way, let your light shine before men, that they may see your good deeds and praise your Father in heaven.

123 Q. What does the second request mean?

A. *Your kingdom come* means,

Rule us by your Word and Spirit in such a way
that more and more we submit to you.[1]

Keep your church strong, and add to it.[2]

Destroy the devil's work;
destroy every force which revolts against you
and every conspiracy against your Word.[3]

Do this until your kingdom is so complete and perfect
that in it you are
all in all.[4]

1   **Ps. 119:5**
Oh, that my ways were steadfast
   in obeying your decrees!

Ps. 119:105
Your word is a lamp to my feet
   and a light for my path.

Ps. 143:10
Teach me to do your will,
   for you are my God;
may your good Spirit
   lead me on level ground.

Matt. 6:33
But seek first his kingdom and his righteousness, and all these things will be given to you as
well.

2   **Ps. 122:6-9**
Pray for the peace of Jerusalem:
   "May those who love you be secure.
May there be peace within your walls
   and security within your citadels."
For the sake of my brothers and friends,
   I will say, "Peace be within you."
For the sake of the house of the LORD our God,
   I will seek your prosperity.

Matt. 16:18
And I tell you that you are Peter, and on this
rock I will build my church, and the gates of
Hades will not overcome it.

Acts 2:42-47
They devoted themselves to the apostles'
teaching and to the fellowship, to the breaking of
bread and to prayer. Everyone was filled with
awe, and many wonders and miraculous signs
were done by the apostles. All the believers were
together and had everything in common. Selling
their possessions and goods, they gave to
anyone as he had need. Every day they continued to meet together in the temple courts.
They broke bread in their homes and ate
together with glad and sincere hearts, praising
God and enjoying the favor of all the people.
And the Lord added to their number daily those
who were being saved.

3   **Rom. 16:20**
The God of peace will soon crush Satan under
your feet.
The grace of our Lord Jesus be with you.

1 John 3:8
He who does what is sinful is of the devil, because the devil has been sinning from the beginning. The reason the Son of God appeared was
to destroy the devil's work.

4   **Rom. 8:22-23**
We know that the whole creation has been
groaning as in the pains of childbirth right up to
the present time. Not only so, but we ourselves,
who have the firstfruits of the Spirit, groan inwardly as we wait eagerly for our adoption as
sons, the redemption of our bodies.

1 Cor. 15:28

When he has done this, then the Son himself will be made subject to him who put everything under him, so that God may be all in all.

Rev. 22:17, 20

The Spirit and the bride say, "Come!" And let him who hears say, "Come!" Whoever is thirsty, let him come; and whoever wishes, let him take the free gift of the water of life.

He who testifies to these things says, "Yes, I am coming soon."

Amen. Come, Lord Jesus.

124 Q. What does the third request mean?

A. *Your will be done on earth as it is in heaven* means,

Help us and all people
to reject our own wills
and to obey your will without any back talk.
Your will alone is good.[1]

Help us one and all to carry out the work we are called to,[2]
as willingly and faithfully as the angels in heaven.[3]

---

1   **Matt. 7:21**

Not everyone who says to me, "Lord, Lord," will enter the kingdom of heaven, but only he who does the will of my Father who is in heaven.

Matt. 16:24-26

Then Jesus said to his disciples, "If anyone would come after me, he must deny himself and take up his cross and follow me. For whoever wants to save his life will lose it, but whoever loses his life for me will find it. What good will it be for a man if he gains the whole world, yet forfeits his soul? Or what can a man give in exchange for his soul?"

Luke 22:42

Father, if you are willing, take this cup from me; yet not my will, but yours be done.

Rom. 12:1-2

Therefore, I urge you, brothers, in view of God's mercy, to offer your bodies as living sacrifices, holy and pleasing to God—this is your spiritual act of worship. Do not conform any longer to the pattern of this world, but be transformed by the renewing of your mind. Then you will be able to test and approve what God's will is—his good, pleasing and perfect will.

Tit. 2:11-12

For the grace of God that brings salvation has appeared to all men. It teaches us to say "No" to ungodliness and worldly passions, and to live self-controlled, upright and godly lives in this present age,

2   **1 Cor. 7:17-24**

Nevertheless, each one should retain the place in life that the Lord assigned to him and to which God has called him. This is the rule I lay down in all the churches. Was a man already circumcised when he was called? He should not become uncircumcised. Was a man uncircumcised when he was called? He should not be circumcised. Circumcision is nothing and uncircumcision is nothing. Keeping God's commands is what counts. Each one should remain in the situation which he was in when God called him. Were you a slave when you were called? Don't let it trouble you—although if you can gain your freedom, do so. For he who was a slave when he was called by the Lord is the Lord's freedman; similarly, he who was a free man when he was called is Christ's slave. You were bought at a price; do not become slaves of men. Brothers, each man, as responsible to God, should remain in the situation God called him to.

Eph. 6:5-9

Slaves, obey your earthly masters with respect and fear, and with sincerity of heart, just as you would obey Christ. Obey them not only to win their favor when their eye is on you, but like slaves of Christ, doing the will of God from your heart. Serve wholeheartedly, as if you were serving the Lord, not men, because you know that the Lord will reward everyone for whatever good he does, whether he is slave or free.

And masters, treat your slaves in the same way. Do not threaten them, since you know that he who is both their Master and yours is in heaven, and there is no favoritism with him.

3   **Ps. 103:20-21**

Praise the LORD, you his angels,
you mighty ones who do his bidding,
who obey his word.
Paise the Lord, all his heavenly hosts,
you his servants who do his will.

173

125 Q. What does the fourth request mean?

A. *Give us today our daily bread* means,

Do take care of all our physical needs[1]
so that we come to know
    that you are the only source of everything good,[2]
    and that neither our work and worry
    nor your gifts
    can do us any good without your blessing.[3]

And so help us to give up our trust in creatures
and to put trust in you alone.[4]

[1]   **Ps. 104:27-30**

These all look to you
  to give them their food at the proper time.
When you give it to them,
  they gather it up;
when you open your hand,
  they are satisfied with good things.
When you hide your face,
  they are terrified;
when you take away their breath,
  They die and return to the dust.
When you send your Spirit,
  they are created,
  and you renew the face of the earth.

Ps. 145:15-16

The eyes of all look to you,
  and you give them their food at the
      proper time.
You open your hand
  and satisfy the desires of every living thing.

Matt. 6:25-34

Therefore I tell you, do not worry about your life, what you will eat or drink; or about your body, what you will wear. Is not life more important than food, and the body more important than clothes? Look at the birds of the air; they do not sow or reap or store away in barns, and yet your heavenly Father feeds them. Are you not much more valuable than they? Who of you by worrying can add a single hour to his life?

And why do you worry about clothes? See how the lilies of the fields grow. They do not labor or spin. Yet I tell you that not even Solomon in all his splendor was dressed like one of these. If that is how God clothes the grass of the field, which is here today and tomorrow is thrown into the fire, will he not much more clothe you, O you of little faith? So do not worry, saying, "What shall we eat?" or "What shall we drink?" or "What shall we wear?" For the pagans run after all these things, and your heavenly Father knows that you need them. But seek first his kingdom and his righteousness, and all these things will be given to you as well. Therefore do not worry about tomorrow, for tomorrow will worry about itself. Each day has enough trouble of its own.

[2]   **Acts 14:17**

Yet he has not left himself without testimony: He has shown kindness by giving you rain from heaven and crops in their seasons; he provides you with plenty of food and fills your hearts with joy.

Acts 17:25

And he is not served by human hands, as if he needed anything, because he himself gives all men life and breath and everything else.

James 1:17

Every good and perfect gift is from above, coming down from the Father of the heavenly lights, who does not change like shifting shadows.

[3]   **Deut. 8:3**

He humbled you, causing you to hunger and then feeding you with manna, which neither you nor your fathers had known, to teach you that man does not live on bread alone but on every word that comes from the mouth of the LORD.

Ps. 37:16

Better the little that the righteous have
  than the wealth of many wicked;

Ps. 127:1-2

Unless the LORD builds the house,
  its builders labor in vain.

Unless the LORD watches over the city,
the watchmen stand guard in vain.
In vain you rise early
and stay up late,
toiling for food to eat—
for he grants sleep to those he loves.

1 Cor. 15:58

Therefore, my dear brothers, stand firm. Let nothing move you. Always give yourselves fully to the work of the Lord, because you know that your labor in the Lord is not in vain.

4   Ps. 55:22

Cast your cares on the LORD
and he will sustain you;
he will never let the righteous fall.

Ps. 62

My soul finds rest in God alone;
my salvation comes from him.
He alone is my rock and my salvation;
he is my fortress, I will never be shaken.

How long will you assault a man?
Would all of you throw him down—
this leaning wall, this tottering fence?
They fully intend to topple him
from his lofty place;
they take delight in lies.
With their mouths they bless,
but in their hearts they curse. *Selah*

Find rest, O my soul, in God alone;
my hope comes from him.
He alone is my rock and my salvation;
he is my fortress, I will not be shaken.
My salvation and my honor depend on God;
he is my mighty rock, my refuge.
Trust in him at all times, O people;
pour out your hearts to him,
for God is our refuge. *Selah*

Lowborn men are but a breath,
the highborn are but a lie;
if weighed on a balance, they are nothing;
together they are only a breath.
Do not trust in extortion
or take pride in stolen goods;
though your riches increase,
do not set your heart on them.

One thing God has spoken,
two things have I heard:
that you, O God, are strong,

and that you, O Lord, are loving.
Surely you will reward each person
according to what he has done.

Ps. 146

Praise the LORD.

Praise the LORD, O my soul.
I will praise the LORD all my life;
I will sing praise to my God as long as I live.

Do not put your trust in princes,
in mortal men, who cannot save.
When their spirit departs, they return to
the ground;
on that very day their plans come to nothing.

Blessed is he whose help is the God of Jacob,
whose hope is in the LORD his God,
the Maker of heaven and earth,
the sea, and everything in them—
the LORD, who remains faithful forever.
He upholds the cause of the oppressed
and gives food to the hungry.
The LORD sets prisoners free,
the LORD gives sight to the blind,
the LORD lifts up those who are bowed down,
the LORD loves the righteous.
The LORD watches over the alien
and sustains the fatherless and the widow,
but he frustrates the ways of the wicked.

The LORD reigns forever,
your God, O Zion, for all generations.

Praise the LORD.

Jer. 17:5-8

This is what the LORD says:

"Cursed is the one who trusts in man,
who depends on flesh for his strength
and whose heart turns away from the LORD.
He will be like a bush in the wastelands;
he will not see prosperity when it comes.
He will dwell in the parched places of the desert,
in a salt land where no one lives.

"But blessed is the man who trusts in the LORD,
whose confidence is in him.
He will be like a tree planted by the water
that sends out its roots by the stream.
It does not fear when heat comes;
its leaves are always green.
It has no worries in a year of drought
and never fails to bear fruit."

Heb. 13:5-6

Keep your lives free from the love of money and be content with what you have, because God has said,

"Never will I leave you;
never will I forsake you."

So we say with confidence,

"The Lord is my helper; I will not be afraid.
What can man do to me?"

126 Q. What does the fifth request mean?

A. *Forgive us our debts,*
as we also have forgiven our debtors means,

Because of Christ's blood,
do not hold against us, poor sinners that we are,
any of the sins we do
or the evil that constantly clings to us.[1]

Forgive us just as we are fully determined,
as evidence of your grace in us,
to forgive our neighbors.[2]

[1]   **Ps. 51:1-7**

Have mercy on me, O God,
according to your unfailing love;
according to your great compassion
blot out my transgressions.
Wash away all my iniquity
and cleanse me from my sin.

For I know my transgressions,
and my sin is always before me.
Against you, you only, have I sinned
and done what is evil in your sight,
so that you are proved right when you speak
and justified when you judge.
Surely I was sinful at birth,
sinful from the time my mother
conceived me.
Surely you desire truth in the inner parts;
you teach me wisdom in the inmost place.

Cleanse me with hyssop, and I will be clean;
wash me, and I will be whiter than snow.

Ps. 143:2

Do not bring your servants into judgment,
for no one living is righteous before you.

Rom. 8:1

Therefore, there is now no condemnation for
those who are in Christ Jesus,

1 John 2:1-2

My dear children, I write this to you so that
you will not sin. But if anybody does sin, we
have one who speaks to the Father in our
defense—Jesus Christ, the Righteous One. He is
the atoning sacrifice for our sins, and not only
for ours but also for the sins of the whole world.

[2]   **Matt. 6:14-15**

For if you forgive men when they sin against
you, your heavenly Father will also forgive you.
But if you do not forgive men their sins, your
Father will not forgive your sins.

Then Peter came to Jesus and asked, "Lord, how many times shall I forgive my brother when he sins against me? Up to seven times?"

Jesus answered, "I tell you, not seven times, but seventy-seven times.

"Therefore, the kingdom of heaven is like a king who wanted to settle accounts with his servants. As he began the settlement, a man who owed him ten thousand talents was brought to him. Since he was not able to pay, the master ordered that he and his wife and his children and all that he had be sold to repay the debt.

"The servant fell on his knees before him. 'Be patient with me,' he begged, 'and I will pay back everything.' The servant's master took pity on him, canceled the debt and let him go.

"But when that servant went out, he found one of his fellow servants who owed him a hundred denari. He grabbed him and began to choke him. 'Pay back what you owe me!' he demanded.

"His fellow servant fell to his knees and begged him, 'Be patient with me, and I will pay you back.'

"But he refused. Instead, he went off and had the man thrown into prison until he could pay the debt. When the other servants saw what had happened, they were greatly distressed and went and told their master everything that had happened.

"Then the master called the servant in. 'You wicked servant,' he said. 'I canceled all that debt of yours because you begged me to. Shouldn't you have had mercy on your fellow servant just as I had on you?' In anger his master turned him over to the jailers to be tortured, until he should pay back all he owed.

"This is how my heavenly Father will treat each of you unless you forgive your brother from your heart."

127 Q. What does the sixth request mean?

A. *And lead us not into temptation,*
but deliver us from the evil one means,

By ourselves we are too weak
to hold our own even for a moment.[1]

And our sworn enemies—
the devil,[2] the world,[3] and our own flesh—[4]
never stop attacking us.

And so, Lord,
uphold us and make us strong
with the strength of your Holy Spirit,
so that we may not go down to defeat
in this spiritual struggle,[5]
but may firmly resist our enemies
until we finally win the complete victory.[6]

[1]   **Ps. 103:14-16**
for he knows how we are formed,
he remembers that we are dust.
As for man, his days are like grass,
he flourishes like a flower of the field;
the wind blows over it and it is gone,
and its place remembers it no more.

John 15:1-5
I am the true vine, and my Father is the gardener. He cuts off every branch in me that bears no fruit, while every branch that does bear fruit he prunes so that it will be even more fruitful. You are already clean because of the word I have spoken to you. Remain in me, and I will remain in you. No branch can bear fruit by itself; it must remain in the vine. Neither can you bear fruit unless you remain in me.
I am the vine; you are the branches. If a man remains in me and I in him, he will bear much fruit; apart from me you can do nothing.

[2]   **2 Cor. 11:14**
And no wonder, for Satan himself masquerades as an angel of light.

Eph. 6:10-13
Finally, be strong in the Lord and in his mighty power. Put on the full armor of God so that you can take your stand against the devil's schemes. For our struggle is not against flesh and blood, but against the rulers, against the authorities, against the powers of this dark world and against the spiritual forces of evil in the heavenly realms. Therefore put on the full armor of God, so that when the day of evil comes, you may be able to stand your ground, and after you have done everything to stand.

1 Pet. 5:8
Be self-controlled and alert. Your enemy the devil prowls around like a roaring lion looking for someone to devour.

[3]   **John 15:18-21**
If the world hates you, keep in mind that it hated me first. If you belonged to the world, it would love you as its own. As it is, you do not belong to the world, but I have chosen you out of the world. That is why the world hates you. Remember the words I spoke to you: "No servant is greater than his master." If they persecuted me, they will persecute you also. If they obeyed my teaching, they will obey yours also. They will treat you this way because of my name, for they do not know the One who sent me.

[4]   **Rom. 7:23**
but I see another law at work in the members of my body, waging war against the law of my mind and making me a prisoner of the law of sin at work within my members.

Gal. 5:17
For the sinful nature desires what is contrary to the Spirit, and the Spirit what is contrary to

the sinful nature. They are in conflict with each other so that you do not do what you want.

5   **Matt. 10:19-20**

But when they arrest you, do not worry about what to say or how to say it. At that time you will be given what to say, for it will not be you speaking, but the Spirit of your Father speaking through you.

Matt. 26:41

Watch and pray so that you will not fall into temptation. The spirit is willing, but the body is weak.

Mark 13:33

Be on guard! Be alert! You do not know when that time will come.

Rom. 5:3-5

Not only so, but we also rejoice in our sufferings, because we know that suffering produces perseverance; perseverance, character; and character, hope. And hope does not disappoint us, because God has poured out his love into our hearts by the Holy Spirit, whom he has given us.

6   **1 Cor. 10:13**

No temptation has seized you except what is common to man. And God is faithful; he will not let you be tempted beyond what you can bear. But when you are tempted, he will also provide a way out so that you can stand up under it.

1 Thess. 3:13

May he strengthen your hearts so that you will be blameless and holy in the presence of our God and Father when our Lord Jesus comes with all his holy ones.

1 Thess. 5:23

May God himself, the God of peace, sanctify you through and through. May your whole spirit, soul and body be kept blameless at the coming of our Lord Jesus Christ.

128 Q. What does your conclusion to this prayer mean?

A. *For yours is the kingdom*
and the power
and the glory forever means,

We have made all these requests of you
because, as our all-powerful king,
　　you not only want to,
　　　but are able to give us all that is good;[1]
and because your holy name,
　　and not we ourselves,
　　should receive all the praise, forever.[2]

1　　　　　**Rom. 10:11-13**

As the Scripture says, "Anyone who trusts in him will never be put to shame." For there is no different between Jew and Gentile—the same Lord is Lord of all and richly blesses all who call on him, for, "Everyone who calls on the name of the Lord will be saved."

2 Pet. 2:9

If this is so, then the Lord knows how to rescue godly men from trials and to hold the unrighteous for the day of judgment, while continuing their punishment.

2　　　　　**Ps. 115:1**

Not to us, O Lord, not to us
　　but to your name be the glory,
　　because of your love and faithfulness.

John 14:13

And I will do whatever you ask in my name, so that the Son may bring glory to the Father.

129 Q. What does that little word "Amen" express?

A. *Amen* means,

This is sure to be!

It is even more sure
    that God listens to my prayer,
than that I really desire
    what I pray for.[1]

1   **Isa. 65:24**

Before they call I will answer;
  while they are still speaking I will hear.

2 Cor. 1:20

For no matter how many promises God has made, they are "Yes" in Christ. And so through him the "Amen" is spoken by us to the glory of God.

2 Tim. 2:13

If we are faithless,
  he will remain faithful,
  for he cannot disown himself.